Ludwig Dehio was born in Königsberg, Prussia, in 1888 and received his degrees from the Universities of Berlin and Strasbourg. In 1922 he began working as an archivist in the Secret State Archives, Berlin-Dahlem, and in 1933 became director of archives of the House of Hohenzollern. From 1946-1954 he was director of the German State Archives at Marburg a/L. He was appointed editor-in-chief of the *Historische Zeitschrift* when it resumed publication in 1948, and he held this position until his retirement in 1956.

GERMANY AND WORLD POLITICS IN THE TWENTIETH CENTURY

By
LUDWIG DEHIO

Translated by
DIETER PEVSNER

The Norton Library
W · W · NORTON & COMPANY · INC ·
NEW YORK

First published in the Norton Library 1967
by arrangement with Alfred A. Knopf, Inc.

Books That Live

The Norton imprint on a book means that in the publisher's
estimation it is a book not for a single season but for the years.
W. W. Norton & Company, Inc.

SBN 393 00391 4

PRINTED IN THE UNITED STATES OF AMERICA

3 4 5 6 7 8 9 0

CONTENTS

NOTE

THE five essays[1] in this volume were originally published separately in the following journals and periodicals: "Germany and the Period of the two World Wars" in *Historische Zeitschrift*, Vol. 173, 1 (1952); "Ranke and German Imperialism" in *Historische Zeitschrift*, Vol. 170, 2 (1950); "Thoughts on Germany's Mission 1900–1918" in *Historische Zeitschrift*, Vol. 174, 2 (1952); "Versailles after Thirty-five Years" in *Der Monat* (July 1954); "The Passing of the European System" in *Aussenpolitik* (June 1953).

[1] The German edition of this book contained a sixth essay which was of ephemeral interest and has been omitted from this translation.

FOREWORD

THE essays published in this book vary in their approach. Some of them are academic studies, while others are a journalist's articles written for particular occasions. The former deal with past events and have a firm historical basis, in the hope that they may achieve some degree of permanence. In the latter, I have taken the risk of trusting myself to the unstable elements of the present. If the reader requires a justification for the presentation of both groups together, he may perhaps find it, first, in the fact that they are all limited in subject to our own country, and secondly in the underlying idea, common to all five, which is the product of my experience of the two German catastrophes and of their effects to this day.

In a previous book, *Gleichgewicht oder Hegemonie*, I tried to show how far the two World Wars should be regarded as links in the chain formed by the wars for European hegemony (from Charles V and Philip II to Louis XIV and Napoleon I) and as the great precursors of the dialectical swing from the pluralism of the West to the dualism of the world of today. In the first three essays in this collection I have tried to develop some important points in the outline that I put forward in that book—especially the controversial question of Germany's part in the events of this century—and to examine whether the way I put the question reveals the essential framework of the course of events. The essay on the Treaty of Versailles also belongs in this

9

group, but at the same time its journalistic approach leads on to the last essay. This deals exclusively with the present, but it nevertheless interprets the present by continually turning back to developments in earlier periods which, like ghosts, continue to affect us, although they are in fact long dead.

At a moment when opinion is wavering between radical rethinking and traditionalism, I hope that these essays, which take both into account, may make a modest contribution to the consolidation of our ideas.

Marburg, July 1955.   LUDWIG DEHIO

GERMANY AND THE PERIOD OF THE TWO WORLD WARS

AFTER years of political passivity, Germany is now returning to a position of independent responsibility.[1] More than ever before she now needs a clear understanding of the period preceding her exclusion from responsibility—that is, the period of the two World Wars. If we are to discuss this period in the limited space available here, we must do so with the brevity of aphorism. I shall merely emphasize a number of points which, if linked together, may give us a rough outline of events.

Let us begin by advancing a guiding concept—one which seems to me well-suited to serve as the central point of this discussion, or indeed of any discussion that tries to be something more than a mere indictment or defence of events and become an integrated historical account. The concept I have in mind is that of the struggle for hegemony: for the two World Wars, like two consecutive acts of the same drama, both display in their most exaggerated form the familiar generic traits of the great European wars associated with the names of Charles V, Philip II, Louis XIV and Napoleon I.

It would take too much time to support this thesis by a comparative analysis of external events over the whole field of relations between the great European

[1] This essay is a slightly expanded version of a lecture delivered at the Twenty-first Congress of German Historians in September 1951.

11

powers. Let us none the less try to turn this method to advantage in considering the history of Germany, and her internal affairs in particular, in our own age. Here we may profitably advance another concept whose connection with the first can easily be demonstrated—that of the daemonic nature of power. It was no coincidence that this concept impressed itself so forcibly upon our consciousness during the second World War —the last struggle for European hegemony.

In attaching such overwhelming importance to my guiding concept, I depart at the outset from other interpretations which reject that concept, especially those which regard the history of Germany in this period as growing, like a tree, out of purely German roots and which overlook the extent to which German history has been entangled with the history of other nations. I am also departing from those interpretations that take a broader view of events and emphasize contemporary analogies. There is some truth in both these views, but both require amplification. This is especially true of the interpretation (more popular abroad) that isolates Germany. This view tends to over-emphasize Germany's peculiar characteristics, whereas the second view tends to disregard them. Those who acknowledge that Germany has in our time exercised supreme power will avoid both these errors. They will see that, in her role of supremacy, Germany was essentially different from her fellows in the family of nations, but they will not regard this as proof that Germany has always possessed this distinct personality. A consideration of events from a broader point of view will make us cautious in passing judgement; and we can gain that broader point of view by looking back over the history of older powers that have exercised hegemony over Europe. We shall then realize that many of the characteristics of modern Germany which, seen in terms of the twentieth century, impress us as specifically German, have appeared, to some extent at least, among earlier supreme powers. Seen in terms of earlier centuries, these characteristics emerge as typical of all supreme powers, and this comparison with the past also makes us realize how far Germany's two wars have unique significance within the whole series of the wars for hegemony. In the last analysis any comparison, whether with past or present phenomena, only makes this unique significance emerge even more clearly and objectively.

The daemonic nature of power, which drives its victim to an exaggerated desire for self-assertion and to an amoral lust for battle, inevitably appears in its most violent form in the most comprehensive and embittered of all European struggles—the struggles for hegemony. Moreover, since the supreme power stands in the solitude of its supremacy, it must face daemonic temptations of a special kind.

These introductory considerations should suffice. Let us now briefly describe how Germany entered the select circle of European supreme Powers. We find that the central factor in all the struggles for European hegemony (which are our sole concern) is the conflict which develops each time between the strongest power on the old continent (excluding its eastern fringes) and the reigning maritime power. Before the beginning of German naval armament there was never any trace of a conflict of this nature in the history of Prussia and Germany. Both of them displayed all the most distinctive characteristics of the purely continental type of power—though enhanced perhaps by a vehemence and a youthful vigour equalled by no other power at the time. The westward expansion of Prussia thoroughly reinvigorated the flagging nation, while from her eastern fringes, so poor in history and culture, she gained the violent and infectious intensity that evoked and moulded a new vitality—biological, spiritual, economic and, above all, political. At this point we observe that trinity—exceptionally bold leadership, systematic arming and disciplined manpower— which was to make an indelible mark on the thinking of the young German nation. The tradition of the Prussian power state, more attractive than anything which Western civilization had to offer, taught the triumph of the will and the lesson that will-power could carry one with giant strides from the smallest beginnings into the circle of the Great Powers.

The period during which German history was purely continental ended abruptly at the beginning of the present century. We suddenly entered the arena where the most important European and global decisions are made—decisions which, no matter how tremendous the struggle on the continent, are always made at sea, not on land. Let us ask ourselves not what caused the first World War, but what made it possible. The answer is that, as a World War, it was undoubtedly the expansionist pressure of the rejuvenated German nation that made it possible, for Russian expansionist ambitions alone could not at that time have provoked it. But the fact that the war assumed the classic form of a struggle for European hegemony was due to the reactions of Britain.

Just as Prussia had once broken into the ranks of the great European powers, so did we Germans hope to break out of the narrow confines of Europe and join the ranks of the world powers, and we tried to do so by typically Prussian methods: that is, by systematic arming—in this case naval arming. But this was impossible without, as it were, forcing the European system into retirement. Nor was it possible without forcing Britain into retirement—without forcing her out of her role of guarantor of the existing balance of power in Europe and out of her position of maritime supremacy in the world beyond. What was the inevitable result of our efforts? We found ourselves embarked upon the road to World War. We, and we only, threatened the vital nerve centres of British world power. Though otherwise true to type, our imperialism was unique in this respect—despite the fact that the imperialism of other nations produced much more extensive friction with Britain in colonial areas than did our own.

We turned our uncertain gaze on to the wide world, but instead of keeping our eyes firmly on the acquisition of particular territories, we gambled on general changes in the entire *status quo* at the expense of our rival. Meanwhile England sought to maintain herself by defending the traditional European balance of power, which we regarded as almost obsolete because of the position of semi-supremacy occupied on the continent by Bismarck's Reich. By her policy of encirclement England gradually forced us into the isolated position of a potential aspirant for European hegemony in the full sense of the term. At the same time, the aim of German imperialism was still to become

15

one of a circle of world powers, without necessarily destroying English maritime supremacy. Thus each of the rivals was fighting against the position of hegemony occupied by the other and appealing for a balance of power; but each attached a totally different sense to the terms "hegemony" and "balance of power".

Even before 1914 the pressure of encirclement made us doubt whether the optimistic calculations we had made at the turn of the century would prove right. We had thought that England would be held in check by our naval armament and would allow herself to be peacefully manœuvred out of her key positions. But the descisive fact was that, in our youthful exuberance, we failed to draw the logical conclusions from our own ideas. In 1913 Plehn could write: "It is an almost universal belief throughout the country that we shall only win our freedom to participate in world politics through a major European war."[1]

So this major European war, which was to become a World War, took place. Now our transformation, hitherto only an impending danger, became a terrible reality. We assumed the role of a power in pursuit of European hegemony. Any attempt by the strongest state on the continent to discard the old balance of power must logically involve an attempt to win European hegemony, however much we might try to disguise the fact from ourselves and others. Now, under the impact of the changed situation, certain entirely new traits appeared in our character. These traits cannot be said to date from an earlier period, though they naturally pre-suppose our earlier history—as a storey added to a house pre-supposes the lower storeys.

[1] In *Deutsche Weltpolitik und kein Krieg*, p. 1.

We shall understand the course of events more easily if we stand aside for a moment and try to consider the typical fate of earlier supreme powers. Each of them played a lonely role of tragic grandeur. Their efforts, deliberate or otherwise, to establish their own predominance touched off all the momentous happenings of the great European wars. In every case these efforts inevitably assumed extreme forms as the other imperilled states united in grand coalitions under the leadership of the island power on the wing. Every time the supreme power was finally forced to fight alone against all the rest. But it dared to fight such a battle, for it was inflated with the self-confidence born of the knowledge that it had reached the supreme moment of its destiny, that it stood head and shoulders above all its neighbours. No care or danger could restrain it; these only stimulated its exuberant sense of power into seizing the hour of greatness before it passed. It was lured on to win the prize of a new level of self-fulfilment and power far higher than that of all its enemies, who at first simply struggled to maintain the positions that they already held. But as soon as the supreme power reached the point where it came into conflict with the island power and faced a grand coalition, the solid ground of its continental experience and its *raison d'état* disappeared from under its feet. At this point the first characteristic feature—power— is joined by a second—blindness in the use of power. The combination of the two characteristics finally produces the daemonic nature to which, as we have noted, any supreme power is prone. Not that the intensity of the struggle does not also unleash among the other powers daemonic forces varying according to their different traditions and situations. In them, however, these daemonic forces are to some extent mere reactions; they lack the two characteristic factors which would intensify them to their ultimate degree. This is especially clear in the case of the island power. Its *raison d'état* has specially strong foundations in wars for hegemony, and its resources, carefully controlled by its traditional wisdom, only grow to full strength in the course of the conflict. Its adversary across the channel always has the characteristics of a new-comer, neither inheriting the experience of a predecessor nor passing on his own to succeeding generations. In spite of well-planned military preparations, his giant strength is sapped by hurried improvisation, because he lacks any well-prepared political plans wherewith to control it. Naturally his aim is complete and final victory in order to give his achievements all possible permanence; but as this victory slips from his grasp, he sees his work reduced to ruins before it is even finished. Thus, in spite of variations, a single pattern of events has been repeated more and more clearly over the centuries. At the beginning of the struggle the supreme power reaches the culmination of its previous history, and its initial successes form a magnificent, triumphant, clear-cut crystallization of its nature. But as the struggle drags wearily on intense euphoria turns into daemonic excess. The screws are turned too tight. Finally, the rulers, like gamblers with no real understanding of the game they are playing, stake their fundamental material and moral values. Their hopes flare up until the last moment, only to lure them on to their ultimate fall.

This typical course, which each supreme power

altered and exaggerated in its own peculiar fashion, characterized Germany's development during the first World War—with this difference that, threatening and threatened by all and sundry, the essentially unprepared Central Powers played their role on a contracting and sinking continent and in the explosive atmosphere of a more advanced civilization; and that the whole development was thus swifter, more violent and more destructive then ever before. This time, all the heights and all the depths were touched, not in the course of decades but in a matter of years. In 1914, confronted with the hatred of "a whole world of enemies", we experienced an intoxicating intensification of our whole being; but this sudden spiritual isolation, which was the result of our political isolation, contained the seeds of excess. This development, foreseen only by a few thoughtful men, was hastened by the accumulated emotions of the majority. It shattered the spiritual balance of the nation. Encircled by hatred, the people replied with its own hatred. Society and the machinery of state were overstrained by the lonely and glorious, but ill-fated struggle, and traditions were distorted. Extremist and monomaniac ideas, which might have remained mere marginal phenomena in a calmer context, began to spread.

It is arresting to observe how the more clear-sighted tried to break this vicious circle by consulting the oracle of the *raison d'état* governing our internal policies; but the oracle's obscure replies only increased the confusion. The Seven Years War had not been a war for hegemony, and the strategy of attrition on land lost its meaning as soon as our opponent began to gain the upper hand with his policy of attrition at sea. In spite of their admirable restraint, even those who favoured a negotiated peace could not tear one last veil from their eyes. Even they underestimated their island foe. Moreover, they occasionally let slip some extremely sinister ideas: for example, Max Weber's words: "Let them hate us, as long as they fear us"; or Otto Hintze's threat: "If the worst comes to the worst, we shall let ourselves be buried beneath the ruins of European civilization."

Words like these pointed to the future; but on the whole it is true to say that the daemonic nature of German aspirations to supremacy only reached its first stage in the first World War. Although it had begun to undermine the whole structure of existing society, of morality, and of the historic state and its traditions, it had not as yet shattered that structure; but the normal forces of civilization were eroding its foundations in any case. These daemonic forces were still loyalist, not revolutionary; and to that extent they recalled the struggles of the Spanish and French monarchs, rather than those of the French Revolution and Napoleon.

There was a complete change in the first years of the peace. The daemonic nature of German aspirations to hegemony reached its second stage. How could this unexpected development come about? Why did the catastrophe of 1918 not, on the contrary, have a sedative effect? To answer these questions we must consider both what happened to Germany as a nation, and what happened inside Germany.

The end of every earlier war for hegemony had established peace for generations. But how could the victors of 1919 possibly establish a lasting peace with the old prescriptions? This had still been possible in 1815, when a peace was made that was severe yet reconciliatory. This time, however, the very foundation underlying earlier peace treaties—the European system—had been severely damaged. On the one hand, Russia had been forced out of the system, becoming at the same time a graver danger to the West than ever; on the other hand, America had been drawn in, for Europe had, for the first time, proved unable to master the threat of hegemony by its own efforts. How could anything lasting be created in so confused a situation? To start with, a solution might only be possible in the West; and even then not without the participation of America, the decisive military power of the West, nor without some new creative idea. Wilson was the bearer of such an idea. What he proposed was not a renewal of the European system with its wars for hegemony, nor the establishment of a world system with its corresponding dangers. Instead he proposed the total abolition of foreign policy in the old sense of the term: that is, the total abolition of a multitude of sovereign states, each ready to wage war; and he proposed in their place the peaceful unification of the nations into a worldwide commonwealth under Anglo-Saxon leadership. What a fantastic transformation! Or was it to remain in the realm of fantasy? Hitherto the insular way of life, represented by England, had been the traditional opponent of any new-comer on the continent. This insular attitude was now represented by America, herself a new-comer. At the time, her ideas seemed almost absurdly simple-minded to European statesmen; but to the people they seemed like a new gospel, and to the German people, in particular, they meant a release

21

from their constriction by means of the peaceful neutralization of the old suffocating system, and so a miraculous solution of the whole German problem.

But the danger to our shattered spiritual balance became even greater, for the miracle remained a dream. On the heels of the catastrophe of the war came the catastrophe of the peace. Old Europe had its way against the new-comer America, and the obsolete European system was roughly patched up. Europe stood on the threshold of a new age, but it stepped back, not forward. This in itself is the most significant explanation of the disaster to come. Within the narrow framework of the weakened European system, the great German problem could be solved neither by severity nor by kindness. There were no powers on the continent to provide the kind of natural counter-balance to the defeated supreme power that had been the basis of the great peace settlements of the past. Instead, even severer conditions were to be imposed, far exceeding any made before, and Germany was to be artificially shackled. But the political and psychological situation underwent a rapid change. The solid front of the Western victors crumbled away. Public opinion in the world shamefacedly turned its back on the hard conditions that it had only just demanded, and now condemned France, who found herself isolated and tried in vain to make up for the Anglo-Saxon guarantee, out of which she had been cheated by the withdrawal of America, by violently exploiting the terms of the Treaty. France was dominated by an instinctive fear of a German counter-attack as strong as Bismarck's fear of a French counter-attack after 1871.

The peace treaty was a strange and contradictory

concoction of idealistic principles and highly realistic clauses. It did not conciliate the defeated nations by the opportunities it offered or at least permitted, nor, for lack of a united front among the victors, was it really severe. If Germany retained any will to resist, how could such a treaty have anything but a provocative effect on her? By reverting to the obsolete European system, the victors were bound to create at least a danger that the defeated power might revert to the obsolete spirit of the struggle for hegemony.

Whether or not Germany were to revert depended on the interplay of all the external influences upon the domestic life of our nation. If we recall the condition of previous supreme powers during the humiliation that followed their defeat, we find that they remained relatively calm for some time, partly because of their exhaustion after decades of war and partly because they appreciated and developed the considerable opportunities still available to them. The delusions that are part of the daemonic desire for hegemony remained and bred pretensions, resentments and dreams of revenge; but a society that survives defeat has no energy left for a serious resumption of the great struggle, nor any need to make daring leaps in the dark. None of this, however, was true of Germany after 1918. In her case both elements in the daemonic desire for supremacy remained effective—both the delusions and the sense of power. Resentment and dreams of revenge therefore found fruitful soil in Germany; and in addition there was the notable stimulus of misery and the resulting progressive dissolution of traditional social conditions.

Delusions kept us from any sober recognition of the

true causes of our failure, exactly as they had kept France in 1815. In spite of the flood of criticism of details, no critical analysis was made during the post-war years of our limited possibilities in the realm of power politics, just as none had been made during the war or in the period of encirclement before the war. We refused to tear the last bandage from our eyes. We refused to allow the glorious memory of the heroic climax of our modern history to be dulled, or to abandon our hopes of re-establishing our position. It was felt that the catastrophe must have had some unnatural cause. The defeat was ascribed to the seductions and deceits of our enemies, and to errors and treason at home. Public opinion still did not appreciate the illuminating analogies with earlier wars for hegemony, nor the role of sea power, nor the peculiar resources of our island foe. The intervention of America was completely misunderstood; and no wonder, for before long the Americans themselves treated their entry into the war as the effect of mere propaganda and a scramble for gain. Few people realized that a genuine *raison d'état* —America's interest in preventing the unification of Europe under a single power because of the possible threat to areas overseas—contributed to this development. So, paradoxically, when we thought back on the war, our main reaction was a greater, not a lessened, self-confidence. We became increasingly aware of our strength as a nation and we found, almost as much to our own surprise as to the world's, that we had preserved this strength. What could not have been achieved under leaders certain of their aims? We brooded over our defeat, but in order to prove to ourselves that it was undeserved, not to understand why it was deserved. Our aim was to prove that it was the result of a number of avoidable errors, not of fundamental ideas that had been exaggerated.

Meanwhile the post-war years proved that, in spite of all that had happened, our strength as a nation was still much greater than that of the other nations of the old continent of Europe. A glance at previous centuries shows quite clearly that French power had been far more profoundly shattered at the beginning of the nineteenth century, and Spanish power at the beginning of the seventeenth, than had ours at the beginning of the twentieth. Although this fact was a measure of the opportunities open to us despite the magnitude of our disaster, the speed of our recovery to the point where we could start a new struggle for hegemony would nevertheless be incomprehensible in the absence of the stimulus of our economic misery.

At first the people's real determination to fight inevitably gave way to total exhaustion; but small, scattered, illegal groups rekindled the spirit in preparation for infiltration and counter-attack. In our nation of soldiers it found support in the memory of the heroic tragedy of the war, as it had in France after 1815. Now, as then, the disillusioned heroism of "the despised" and of the uprooted turned into burning hatred not only of enemies abroad, but also of those at home. It has been said that after 1815 France was split into two nations looking up to two flags—the victors and the vanquished of Waterloo—and one could maintain that Germany was in a similar state after 1919. The only difference was that, in our case, and because of the different rhythm of our history, our national vitality tended towards Restoration, not Revolution. Not that this made us reject revolutionary methods, or indeed any other methods. Idealism and crime joined forces and the nihilistic will to power prepared the way for the ruthless destruction of the ethical system of the West.

At first the full consequences of this trend were grasped only by small bands of pioneers. But given the chaotic instability of the masses, even small groups of fanatics could achieve a great deal. The pendulum of public opinion began to swing back with a vengeance. The origins of the German Republic were quite different from those of the Third Republic in France and the new Russian Republic. The German Republic was born of the momentary exhaustion of old energies, not from an upsurge of new ones; not of resistance to the foreigner, but of surrender to him. In this it resembled the Bourbon restoration of 1815, with its lack of any contemporary nationalist aura, even though—unlike the Bourbons—it could not point proudly to a great past. Moreover, while the Bourbon régime had been supported by the victors' moderation, the Weimar régime was hampered by the inhumanity of Versailles and clearly displayed the impurity of its birth. Soon a third, extremely dangerous factor—the social disintegration that resulted from misery in its many forms —was added to the two already mentioned. With the loss of national status went a loss of social status. In their competition with Communism, the nationalist activists profited from the influx of desperate men and, like the Communists, gambled on the collapse of the entire Western order established in 1919. Their ideas were a blend between the attractive Prussian (and then German) tradition of power, torn out of its native sociological soil, and formless, revolutionary violence.

Thus the new dynamism of Fascism came into being. A further factor, reinforcing this dynamism, was the racial irredentism which now flowed in from beyond the frontiers of Germany—a great flood of popular passions, and one which could never have occurred under the authoritarian Prussian, and later German, state.

Might the final disaster have been averted by splitting up heavy industry and the great landed estates into smaller units, as so many present-day critics of the Germany of that time believe? Whatever the answer, the result would have been an increase in the number of *déclassés* and even greater economic instability. Property tends to act as a sedative, while those without property have everything to gain and nothing to lose. Furthermore, the nationalist spirit had long since ceased to be a prerogative of the propertied class. Nationalism can inflame a disorganized society more dangerously than it can a solid, settled one; indeed it may be that nationalism cannot really grip the middle and lower classes until the moment when it begins to lose its hold on the upper class. Even the abolition of the monarchy had been a two-edged measure, for it had resulted in a loss of focus. So the rise of the new Caesarism in Italy, which oscillated between Restoration and Revolution and undertook to fill the vacuum with a new authority, stirred up even greater turmoil in Germany. But in Germany its hour had not yet come. Nevertheless, our activists could console themselves with the knowledge that in the long run they had greater opportunities to spread their ideas in Germany than in any other country. In Germany everyone, especially the ex-soldiers, longed to see the stain of the catastrophe expunged—a catastrophe such as only our nation with its aspirations to hegemony, and no other, had ever experienced.

Of course, it was no longer any use seeking revenge at sea. However, in the balkanization of some of our neighbours, in the isolation of France, and especially in the bolshevization of that fateful and enigmatic land, Russia, the catastrophe itself had opened up promising prospects close at hand on the continent. Russia could serve Germany's recovery either as a friend (as Seeckt believed) or (as Ludendorff thought) as an enemy.

This programme of recovery was supported almost unanimously by all the parties. Its points were the restoration of our Eastern frontiers and the *Anschluss* with Austria. Its aims were not merely to re-establish what had existed before, but to follow the failure of *kleindeutsch* maritime expansion with *grossdeutsch* expansion on the continent; to complete the national unification of which the youthful nation had dreamed in 1813 and 1848, when it was still on the threshold of its terrible destiny; to meet a mortal threat by vigorous expansion, and, finally, to rise to a degree of greatness such as no other nation in Europe, least of all France in her senility, could achieve. In other words, the aim was to achieve the firm continental basis that, according to the critics of the time, Wilhelm II should somehow have secured before launching into world politics.

How could this programme be realized? With England's help against France? With the help of the East against the West? Or by wavering between East and West? In any case, it could hardly be realized except through the complete destruction of the order established in 1919.

Within the restricted framework of the moribund system of Versailles, the largest and most vigorous people in Europe could only be temporarily shackled, never permanently pacified.

Yet Europe was still granted the ray of sunshine of Locarno. But she owed this to the return of America more than to her own insight or strength. America's comings and goings had already begun to exercise enormous influence on the ebb and flow of events in Europe. The happy interlude of these years seemed like an antithesis to the years after 1919, when America had left Europe. Then there had followed five years of disorganization: now there was a promising basis for reorganization, even though the return of the United States was perhaps due to economic rather than political reasons. Stresemann's successes must be understood in terms of the solid gold foundations of American loans. But the effect of these loans was strictly limited. The German daemons only retreated a little way. They had no thanks for the liberator of the Rhineland. Moreover, the Americans for their part were careful not to opt clearly for the West, for this would have lent support to the irredentist programme. Instead, they sought freedom of movement between East and West. All the wonderful plans for a European union remained a beautiful dream. The nations of Europe have been brought up to mutual mistrust and violence by their modern system—and this is what was restored in 1919. They seem able to hold together only in one event: when a member of their own circle tries to achieve hegemony.

This one event was soon to occur again. For the French it was a terrible confirmation of their prophecies, but to most Anglo-Saxons it was unexpected. As late as the time of Locarno, T. E. Lawrence, an observer who knew the world so well, had ventured the prediction that, after Spain, France and Germany, it might now be Russia's turn to try to dominate the world from the continent. He could not know that Germany would once more summon up the strength and determination to move into the centre of the stage of world affairs in her old role of a power seeking European hegemony, before Russia stepped on to the same stage to create the new role of a power seeking world hegemony.

Characteristically, the great turning-point in Germany was the result of a new turn of events in America. During the world economic crisis, America withdrew across the sea a second time and thus left the entire Western world in even profounder disorganization than after her first withdrawal. This was the signal that started Germany on her impatient race for revenge. In the confusion Germany saw that the road was clear, as though an earthquake had broken down all barriers. The first German war for hegemony had grown organically out of a period of wealth and prosperity. The second was born of misery and fear. The first had been a mere opening skirmish: the second came to be a well-directed counter-attack from deep in the rear. The great gamble on the disintegration of the Western bourgeois world—the secret aim of both the Fascist and the Communist storm troops—now paid magnificent dividends, both in international and national politics. In international politics Germany's warders, the large and small powers of the shrunken European system, turned out to be cowardly or irresponsible, helpless or short-sighted. France, eager for peace, seemed crippled in the face of the very real danger—one which had long occupied her imagination and which had been accelerated by her own earlier policy. At the same time she was inhibited by her awful experience in the Ruhr and by the attitude of her English ally. Should she have used the rifle in her hand to avoid disaster by resorting to force—in accordance with the provisions of the Treaty which, by now, had been criticized so much? The effects of intervention in national troubles are incalculable. Alternatively, would Churchill's proposal to maintain the unilateral disarmament of Germany as a precautionary measure have created a really healthy situation? Even to raise the question is to show that the answer is not necessarily affirmative. But it was in national politics that the gamble really paid. Even the phenomena of social dissolution that had appeared ten years before had strengthened the activists. This dissolution now drove millions from every class into their arms. If the international guarantees and alliances of the democratic world failed, then only a return to the old, well-worn path of national success could bring salvation— the path to a policy of authority at home and power abroad. Under this magical sign the miraculous transformation of fear into confidence, of social dissonance into social harmony, was successfully achieved. The fact that Germany's recovery took the form of Caesarism rather than legitimism was due to the general atmosphere. Outside Germany, Caesarism had already proved its capacity to rally national feelings in times of crisis and provide a third form of government between predatory Communism and the confused bourgeoisie. Let us be quite clear at this point that, just as imperialism had acquired the additional character of a movement for hegemony when adopted by Germany before 1914, so Caesarism was now deliberately and logically transformed. The German dictator, for whose charismatic leadership the imperialists had themselves secretly hoped, grew into an infinitely larger figure than his peers in other European countries (except Russia). His methods, though possibly modelled on methods practised elsewhere in the West, reached unprecedented heights of horror. The "movement" of those infused with daemonic aspirations to hegemony won every position of power and authority; but the seizure of power did not sober it, as had been expected by so many of those who cheered it on. On the contrary, success raised this daemonic nature to a still higher pitch and forced it violently through the fevered nation's bloodstream. The daemonic was concentrated in Hitler, and through him it spread as it had never done before. He was the very incarnation of the daemon of the total struggle for hegemony. Indeed, so far as can be judged, he was the essential prerequisite for the final outbreak of that struggle. Germany could not conceivably have raised herself to such dizzy heights yet again without the aid of some Satanic genius. Hitler felt himself carried along by the dark wave of the crisis and by the expanding forces of civilization, which threatened to shatter the narrow, obsolete system of states. Moreover, he was continually spurred on by the world-wide aspirations of the Bolsheviks, his much admired rivals. His almost Jacobin reliance on his totalitarian power at home led him to believe that there was nothing he could not achieve outside Germany too. Like a sleep-walker, he clambered between chasms along paths that nobody else could have found, using the conflict between East and West as cover until the moment when he emerged as a third force endangering both, and so united them against him. Thus the same abyss opened that had swallowed both the French Emperor and the German Kaiser. The events of earlier wars for hegemony were repeated, but on a higher level. Once again, victories on the old continent were followed by collapse when Germany was faced with the moral and material resources of the islanders, which she could not understand. Moreover this time, by subordinating their differences to the struggle for survival, the islanders were able to keep the Russian sword in the battle. In 1945 the daemon of the wars for European hegemony claimed its final victim. Germany suffered a catastrophe as total and as terrible as the extent and exercise of her power had been until the very last moment; for, anticipating his own downfall, the nihilistic daemon sent as many into the abyss before him as his last reserves of strength allowed.

This is a brief and hurried survey, but we must not stop here. We must add some closing thoughts and so complete the train of ideas that we foreshadowed in our introductory remarks.

We have seen how Germany's vitality has always driven her beyond the typical in any situation—first in the age of imperialism and then in the age of Caesarism—and how, both times, she met the isolated fate of a supreme power. We have also observed how her role, though unique in terms of the present, displayed certain typical traits when seen within the broader framework of the past. It remains for us to ask what special significance the two links of Germany's wars for supremacy had in the whole chain of the wars for European hegemony. The answer can be reduced to a single sentence. The German struggle was the last of the series. We cannot imagine that it will ever be resumed from the territory of the old continent of Europe. For those who accept this prognosis, the special significance of the two World Wars emerges with absolute precision and compelling logic, even if they are examined within the broader framework of the recent history of Europe. When they are seen in this light, it becomes impossible to classify them as mere individual variations of the previous wars, though they are this too. This is because they also served as the catalyst for a new alignment of forces in the world, and although this situation had been developing gradually since the eighteenth century, it was new for all that. Indeed, the rivalry between the Russians and the Anglo-Saxons in the struggle for world hegemony could not become a reality until 1945, when the final struggle for European hegemony had been decided. Then it was as if their rivalry was given the right of way. The unification of Europe under German hegemony threatened the world powers in their territories overseas and forced them to shelve their differences and unite to defeat Germany (and, for related reasons, Japan). Once they had successfully achieved this end, the modern history of Europe in its old form was finished and the old continent ceased to be the all-important centre of world events. The road was clear for a new phase in history—world history.

The significance of the German struggle for hegemony may be expressed in the following terms. It developed both the material and the spiritual forces of destruction to a higher degree than had any of its predecessors. In the final stages of the struggle, these forces not only turned against the supreme power, the sinking aggressor, as they had always done before; to an unprecedented extent their effects were also felt in every corner of the world. Thanks to the technological powers of our civilization, they wrought unparalleled destruction in human life and achievement, and thanks to terrorism and propaganda, which our civilization has made ubiquitous, they corroded and poisoned the soul of Western man. In this way these forces so weakened the resources of the old continent that, since then, the world powers have completely overshadowed it. The European system, like the power that had pitted itself against it, split in two. The fall of Germany liberated the peoples of Western Europe from the danger of totalitarianism; but, on the other hand, the peoples of Eastern Europe were now exposed to it with a vengeance. This, too, was ultimately a result of the German urge to achieve power, whatever the more specific reasons may have been. Furthermore, it undid the results of the first World War. In 1918 Max Weber had tried to console himself with the outcome of that war by remarking that, in spite of everything, Germany could boast that she had saved Europe from the Russian knout. Even this boast was robbed of all force by the events of 1939. Finally, the second World War accelerated the fall of the West from its tottering position of mastery over the coloured peoples—with unpredictable consequences.

But we must press on. The great wars of the past had all had a fruitful as well as a frightful aspect. They were fought in periods of vigorous civilizations. The supreme powers developed positive intellectual missions—as champions of the Counter-Reformation, as living examples of the aristocratic way of life, or as heralds of the achievements of the Revolution. Even the fight against them produced a spiritual revival. But can we find any trace of this redeeming feature in the German struggle, especially in its last phase? Our exaggerated daemonic drive for power—our desperate protest against the course of events in the world outside, which we did not understand—could not evolve any mission with which to win over other nations. Our ideology of national Caesarism could not be exported. It began to lose its appeal as it became increasingly obvious that the freedom of other nations was being threatened in its name, and as it began increasingly to use Bolshevik methods. When it reached agreement with Bolshevism in 1939, it finally lost all its appeal: that was suicide.

But—to ask a further question—did we not lack any idea capable of winning others over to our side, even in the first World War? No argument can alter the fact that in the youthful German nation the spread of Prussianism resulted in a profounder split between the sphere of power and the sphere of the spirit than existed in the older nations. Even our imperialists had been embarrassed when they had tried to provide some spiritual justification for the expansion of German power. They turned for help to our age of spiritual fulfilment and to its glorification of the individual. They declared that our real mission was to protect the individuality and diversity of the nations against the uniformity of Anglo-Saxon society and Russian bureaucracy. However, this mission automatically ceased to be convincing when in the first World War we were obviously forced into Napoleon's footsteps, whereas the ideals that we were invoking were the ideals of Napoleon's adversaries. Our attempts to use these ideas to justify our expansion towards European hegemony involved an inner contradiction.

On two occasions, Germany has produced ideas that have spread: the Reformation and Marxism. But neither contributed anything to German politics.

To sum up, these two wars were not only infinitely more destructive than previous wars; they were also without their beneficent redeeming features. At least, that is how we see them today. But what will be the verdict of future generations? One day they will perhaps be able to find redeeming features in a renaissance of the spirit of the West and in the establishment of a new political order in the greater West. Will our nation too play a part in such a creative resistance to the corrosive forces of destruction? Many Germans will not cease to hope so. But even though others may have different hopes for the future, the prerequisite for any really creative German response after the period of the two World Wars is the unconditional recognition of the terrible role that we have played in this period. We were the last, and the most daemonic, power to exercise hegemony over the declining old continent of Europe.

RANKE AND GERMAN
IMPERIALISM[1]

HISTORIOGRAPHY has, in general, played
a far more important role in the development
of the less mature nations of Central Europe,
who strove to achieve spiritual and political self-
realization after the great revolution, than it did in
the growth of those Western nations who had long
been sure of their individual nature and form. This
was specially true of Germany and more specially of
Germany during the nineteenth century. But in the
course of the century, and under the influence of its
major political events, the role of historiography clearly
underwent some subtle changes, and three periods can
be approximately distinguished. First, there is the
period before March 1848, when Ranke expounded his
impartial Olympian and universal view of history. The
decades from 1848 until the beginning of Bismarck's
Reich constitute a second period when an eager participation in the remoulding of the German nation had
the effect of limiting the themes of historiography

[1] I have not found it easy to hand this study over to the publisher. I am afraid that some people may consider it arrogant. In
actual fact, I have never ceased to feel grateful and indebted to the
great men of past generations. Indeed, I feel that I am fulfilling
the spirit of their intentions in exploiting the new viewpoint we
have gained today from the heap of rubble that is our experience.
I am, moreover, conscious how much I myself have changed
between the days of our ambitious pursuit of national power
before 1914, and the present.

and infusing them with new warmth. The last period presents a changed picture, and it is to this picture that the present study is devoted. It is a period determined by the rise of a generation for which the newly created Reich was secure and permanent, and its creator and the political leadership in general were the objects of a settled confidence. Once this generation had accepted the new authoritarianism as an accomplished fact, it turned its attention outwards and, from its securely established German base, began to observe the thrilling play of forces among the great powers, which Bismarck's diplomatic artistry had successfully controlled on so many occasions. But in the last resort this was only a continuation of the play of forces that had existed ever since the birth of the European system. And who could have been better equipped to interpret its nature from its history than the historiographer of the great powers, old Ranke himself? Over the heads of the intervening generation, the third generation discovered the master, who was still living in their midst. He had already raised the broad structure of his work to impressive heights before the storm of nationalist passions, which had abated somewhat after the foundation of the Reich, began to rage once again. He had conceived his views in an atmosphere of securely established state authority and, to some extent, such an atmosphere developed again after 1870. Among the young historians Ranke's ideas, and with them something of his authoritarian mentality, rose to the surface once more. The state had every cause to be satisfied that an attitude capable of interpreting the actions of its statesmen so favourably should have taken root in the minds of its university professors. It is understandable that the volcanic rhetoric of the most powerful representative of the dying generation, Treitschke, found no real following in the lecture-rooms. However, the burning flood of that generation had already inflamed the educated and semi-educated classes, and had done so with far more permanent effect than the academic world was prepared to admit:[1] but then, in a changing society, the universities were in any case losing some of their extensive influence.

In the nineties, while Ranke's views were spreading wider and wider, Germany's external position also began to take on a new and extremely promising aspect. Under Bismarck this position had been determined by Russian pressure on Central Europe, which had in turn always encouraged a corresponding pressure from France. Then it was the Balkan conflicts that held the world in suspense; later the fear of centripetal co-operation between Germany's eastern and western neighbours was dispelled by their centrifugal activities in the expanses of Africa and Asia. This development stirred England, the old world power, into activity. In competition with her growing rivals, she made even more vigorous efforts to expand. Moreover, in the outside world, the expansion of the three essentially European powers came into conflict with the corresponding activities of the two non-

[1] W. Bussmann's important essay "Treitschke als Politiker" in *Historiche Zeitschrift*, Vol. 177, II, shows clearly that Treitschke, with his idealistic preludes to German imperialism, also influenced the younger generation of scholars, even though he did not form any school of historians. This essay on Ranke and German Imperialism could well have been preceded by one on Treitschke and German Imperialism. The intellectual dove-tailing between the two would have been as instructive as the points of difference.

European powers, the U.S.A. and Japan. The result was that world affairs drove European affairs out of their central position in the public eye. However, Germany, hitherto so uncomfortably confined, now began to breathe more freely and her pulse to beat more exuberantly. Could it be that her position in Europe was now sufficiently secure to allow her to apply the pent-up energies of her vigorous, youthful civilization to world politics, and to continue the rise of the Reich beyond purely continental achievements and on to the level occupied by the older powers? It seemed as if the screens confining her to the continent had been pushed aside, and that the late-comer was at last to be allowed to look out upon the world beyond. So ambitions were formed in the late nineties that were to stand like guiding images before Germany's self-confident embarkation into imperialism.

In giving substance to these images, the important task of making the future that we hoped for grow organically out of the past fell to the historians. It could be fulfilled most easily by the primitive heirs of Treitschke's spirit, especially by the Pan-Germans; for, from their passionate, self-glorifying point of view, the history of their own people was so much more important than any other past events that, in their eyes, our recent splendid development seemed to point the way to higher things and, almost naturally, to guarantee the prospect of a corresponding expansion into world politics. However, our concern is to examine the finer web formed by the ideas of those men who had opened their minds to the spirit of Ranke; for it was they who could really claim to be the legitimate representatives of German scholarship. They strove to avoid naïve

impulsiveness and to emulate instead the thoughtful-
ness of their master, who had always known how to
interpret the fate of each nation in the more general
context of the whole family of nations. He had shown
how, down the centuries of modern history, a majority
of the European powers had always succeeded in maintaining a system of balance and in defeating the
aspirations to hegemony of any single nation. Might
one not draw the conclusion, from this course of events,
that the same development would take place on the
global stage as on the European? It could be said of
Ranke's followers that they were throwing a great
bridge from the peaceful days of Ranke's lifetime into
the crowded age of modern imperialism, and that, with
this apparently solid structure, they were giving the
German cultural élite the welcome impression that the
new policies did not in fact lead beyond the realms of
previous experience and so could not possibly be a
reckless embarkation upon a Sicilian expedition.

The first man to move in this direction, supported
both by the respect inspired by his chair in Berlin and
by the force of his strong yet serene personality, was
Max Lenz. His secular, programmatical views, published in 1900 under the title *Die grossen Mächte*,
found such a lively echo that, soon after their first
appearance in the *Deutsche Rundschau*, they were published as a book. The very title proclaims the work of
a Ranke *epigone*, and the author describes himself as
such, proudly, yet modestly. He seeks to project into
the present, and into the world politics of imperialism, the ideas contained in the master's essay of the
same title—an essay whose significance the author has
felt anew and demonstrates to his readers with dog-

matic confidence. He does so, however, without raising
the question whether experience in Europe can claim
to be valid in the world beyond. On the contrary, it
seems inevitable to Lenz that, just as national risings
had ultimately determined the fate of Europe in the
Napoleonic era, so in his own age the fate of the world
was determined by national energies. These energies
flowed into existing states, either developing them or
disrupting them—and the great world powers, more
than any others, were threatened with disruption.
Thus the other nationalities in the United States, with
their profound differences in race, language, religion,
customs and civilization, might one day crystallize
alongside the Yankees and aspire to their own forms of
existence within the state, as they had within society.
The Czarist Empire, too, had not yet reached its testing
time; and in a future world war to be fought for
Eastern Asia, it might yet have to prove its ability to
govern the world that now served it. However, the
most enigmatic question mark hung over the British
Empire. After the military failures of the old type of
English mercenary army against the people's army of
the Boers, it might be legitimate to speak of a future
War of English Succession—and in that case, the power
and determination of the mighty colonial empire would
probably be tried in more dangerous circumstances
than any encountered in previous struggles. Since in
Asia and Africa the British were facing the very powers
against which they were protected in Europe by a
belt of water and by their navy, there was a danger
that the conditions of war, hitherto so favourable to
them, might be reversed. Lenz always stresses the
factor of disruption even in his consideration of world

politics, and especially the disruption caused by those elemental national forces which, though sometimes dormant for centuries, can never be completely stifled. If once these forces were to break through into Asia, he says, the white nations would certainly have to stand together to preserve their civilization. (This reminds one of the words the Kaiser spoke at this time about our "most sacred possessions".) However, Lenz does not regard this as a motive for the permanent unification of Europe, but only as confirmation of the familiar pattern of white great powers. He goes on to point out the consequences for German politics. If the tendency towards disruption were to spread through the world in the future, as it had through Europe in the past, then, in the approaching crisis, the very nations that had not so far summoned up all their forces could take new hope—and the German nation was one of these. It had certainly fared badly in the division of the world. But—and here the author raises his voice—it is never too late if one can command the kind of power that can be expressed not only in money and financial values, but also in regiments and battleships. The future would definitely not be determined by battles in the world beyond Europe. The greatest, and the ultimate, decisions would be made in Europe. But Lenz is not frightened by this prospect, for he is confident in the power of German arms. "If we wish it, peace must be preserved among the European powers. We can ordain it. We hold the balance in our hands." Peace had been preserved in Europe in this way from 1871, and it was precisely in this way that the great powers had been forced to transfer their activities to territories beyond Europe. The picture of the world drawn here—an extension of the outline drawn by Ranke—clearly offers a heavily armed Germany many tempting prospects of expansion in other continents and, at the same time, the prospect of at least maintaining herself in Europe.

Max Lenz had great influence as an academic teacher. At about the same time, his friend and contemporary Hans Delbrück, also an influential teacher at the University of Berlin and Treitschke's successor as editor of the *Preussische Jahrbücher*, was spreading similar ideas in educated circles. Moreover, he phrased them in his own peculiar way, with greater fire and optimism—for though he was a figure of great individuality, he was also characteristic of the Wilhelminian age. He was concerned above all to prove to his readers that English world supremacy need not go unchallenged—a point which Lenz had merely suggested as a logical consequence of recent history. He enriched the projection of Ranke's ideas from Europe into the world beyond with an extraordinarily acute comparison. As the biographer of Gneisenau and a specialist in the Napoleonic period he argued as follows.[1] The general movement against England that had developed more and more clearly in the last decades was fundamentally the same as the general rising of the nations against Napoleon I in 1813—with the difference that England had not yet allowed the movement to turn into open war but, under pressure, had retreated step by step from her position of supremacy. Just as the supremacy of France had given place, a hundred years earlier, to a reconstructed concert of great powers with equal

[1] Cf. Delbrück, *Vor und nach dem Weltkriege* (Berlin, 1926), p. 10.

rights, so now England's supremacy would give place to a balance of rival world powers. In Delbrück's work, too, the tendency towards a split into nationalities is a fundamental concept, based on Ranke's apparently immutable fundamental assumption. Moreover, this concept is once again linked with the attractive idea that a well-armed Germany would be able to exploit the opportunities in world politics promised by the expected waning of English power. The images of the Great King, Frederick the Great, and the Great Chancellor were still effective, but now not only regiments were needed, but battleships as well. Germany's naval armament in the Wilhelminian period fitted perfectly with this way of thinking, for it promised to help to destroy English supremacy at sea through the establishment of a world system of states. Nor was this to be only to Germany's advantage; indirectly it would also be to the advantage of all England's other rivals, such as Russia and the U.S.A., France, Japan and Turkey. The existence of so many rivals meant that England, even if she defeated one of them, would face the risk of losing her supremacy at sea to the others. Delbrück is thus in complete agreement with Admiral von Tirpitz's theory of risk. Like the Admiral, he is confident that, at the turn of the century, a well-armed Germany will not lack allies against England in the War of English Succession which his friend Lenz foresaw; and his confidence is reasonable, even if only the parallel between modern England and Napoleonic France is drawn. Just as French supremacy on land had once been destroyed by a coalition, so English supremacy at sea must now face a similar fate. Indeed, at the time of the Boer War, when England had lost so much prestige and roused so much hatred, even a more cautious judge than Delbrück might have hoped that Germany would not have to fight alone if a war broke out with the ageing world power. There certainly seemed to be an instability in diplomatic affairs similar to that which contributed to the rise of Frederick the Great and Bismarck. "Everyone has differences of interest, and interests in common, with everyone else." However—as we well know—in the course of a few years the picture changed and, instead of England, it was Germany who once again experienced the *cauchemar des coalitions* in a far more terrible form than ever before. But did this change make Delbrück re-examine the validity of the premises underlying his interpretation, and correct it? By no means. In spite of Germany's growing isolation he was not prepared to admit any error in his calculations. During the Morocco conference he did once remark angrily that the nations defended themselves much less determinedly against a maritime power than against a continental one, and that they seemed to regard English maritime power as a less imminent threat than German land power; but these painful experiences did not lead to any fundamental revision of his calculations. He defiantly accepted the increasingly gloomy situation. From time to time he said that the rivalry between Germany and England could never be eliminated, for its basis lay in the very nature of things. The best that could be hoped for was that the two Powers might hold one another in check with increased armaments: but that is something quite different from a balance of power. Armaments, he said, were really the best deterrent against war, and it was to armaments that

Europe owed such a long period of peace. In this period this argument was as popular as it was dangerous. We have already seen how Lenz first applied it in 1900—though only to the continent. In the same year, in the preamble to the Navy Act, Tirpitz, with his theory of risk, applied it to the realm of sea power as well—and its sting was now directed against England.

But what would happen if Germany's peaceful offensive, which was a kind of cold war directed against England's position in the world, were one day to lead to a real war—in spite of Wilhelm's navy, which had been set up in accordance with the doctrine of risk? When he considered this prospect, Delbrück was not only afraid of defeat but, even more, of victory.[1] He said, rightly, that it must on no account be Germany's aim to defeat England in a war. A victory over England would be the greatest misfortune that could possibly befall Germany, for then she would indeed be approaching a position of world supremacy and would risk sharing the fate of Charles V, Louis XIV and Napoleon I—defeat by a grand coalition. But had we not already laid ourselves open to this fate by our naval armament? There is, indeed, a terrible confusion of contradictory argument in these ideas. On the one hand Delbrück feels impelled to rivalry with England by his projection of Ranke's view of history on to the world beyond Europe, while on the other he feels that the same view of history, when applied to the European situation, contains a warning against recklessly stirring up this rivalry. We see a rift in his thought and a pointer to his later demand for a negotiated peace with

[1] Cf. Delbrück, *Vor und nach dem Weltkriege* (Berlin, 1926), p. 304.

England. On the whole, however, what predominates is his sanguine belief that English supremacy at sea would wane automatically, without a war, and that a world balance of power would emerge in its place. Nevertheless, a disquieting belief to the contrary stirs beneath the cloak of his confidence. A war might still break out, and then a German victory might set the familiar mechanism of the old European balance of power in motion and direct a grand coalition against the supreme continental power. The new world theme that was emerging might once again be drowned by the old European one. He therefore clings all the more firmly to the hope of a lasting armed peace. In his thoughts on imperialism—and not in his alone—there is a blend of perspicacity and blindness. However, his fear of the effects of a German victory over England is illuminating for another reason. We can see how, like so many Germans, he underestimated the role that English sea power played as an outside support for the European balance of power. This underestimate sprang from Ranke's writings,[1] and it is the unspoken

[1] On this point his history of England is particularly revealing. Diether, in *Leopold von Ranke als Politiker*, p. 494, observed that England's sources of power overseas were not sufficiently appreciated in Germany, although they alone explained the extent of England's contribution to the European balance of power. Even in Ranke's first historical and political notes, made in 1818, the continental interpretation of European history emerges. It is quite clearly visible to the attentive reader in *Die grossen Mächte* and in the conversations with King Max. The letters from England also deserve attention; they show what Ranke saw and what he missed. Delbrück followed Ranke's mode of thought exactly when he drew a parallel between the inevitable disintegration of the empires of Napoleon I and Charlemagne (cf. *Vor und nach dem Weltkriege*, p. 10). Clausewitz took into account only Napoleon's continental wars, never his conflict with the maritime power,

prerequisite for the projection of his concept of the balance of power into the world beyond Europe. Had it been recognized that a sea power, regulating the system from outside, was essential to the functioning of that system, the new system could never have been so confidently expected to work. In spite of our intense preoccupation with the nature of our island rival, our vision was obscured by our continental mentality. This was specially true of Tirpitz. One is continually forced to recognize a fundamental relationship between the ideas of the publicist and those of the Admiral—even if, because of the dichotomy characteristic of his thinking, Delbrück's volatile mind went its own way after the war began. Nevertheless both men had made their mark at the turn of the century under the same star; for Tirpitz too believed—and in his case the belief later became a dogma—that a world balance of power at sea must destroy the European balance and England's privileged position with it; that if, with our naval armament, we entrusted ourselves to this current, allies from among the second-class navies would join us from all sides against the ruling maritime power; and finally, that Germany could not possibly lack allies, since her success would promise success to every other nation striving for freedom.[1] In short, he accepted the familiar wish-image that other followers of Ranke drew with all the rich stylistic equipment they received from their master.

Let us, however, return to the historians and put

England, in which lay his fate. This continental interpretation has had an enormous effect on our military theorists and on the whole of military thought in Germany, including that of Delbrück.

[1] Cf., for example, Tirpitz, *Erinernungen*, p. 154.

our questions to a man very different, in his extreme
reserve, from the controversial publicist Delbrück.
What was Otto Hintze's attitude to the problem with
which we are concerned? His earliest answer is given
in his essay on Imperialism and World Power, published in 1907. This essay leads us over ground familiar
to us, which must also have been familiar to the
author for many years. Although the repercussions of
Moroccan politics had already made the danger of encirclement quite apparent, Hintze continued to apply
his mind more and more intensively to the projection
of the European system on to the world outside. He
considered that the aim of modern imperialism should
not be to create a world empire, such as that of the
Romans, but to allow the co-existence of a number of
world powers in a balance of power similar to the
balance of the great powers in the old European system.
The European system was to be replaced by a new
world system of states. Which powers would assert
themselves within it as the great powers of the future
would depend on their economic and political energies.
Germany was not attempting to achieve world hegemony; she was merely trying to ensure a balance of
power in this future world system of states. Moreover,
she could reasonably hope to fulfil this ambition, for the
development that had gradually led to the formation of
the Pentarchy in the seventeenth and eighteenth centuries—and this is reminiscent of Ranke's essay on the
Great Powers—corresponded to the political movements of the present more than did any other pheno-
menon in the earlier history of the great powers. With
the aid of her navy and her economy, England had
been able to create for herself a privileged position in

the world after 1815, and some of her politicians and patriots hoped that, in co-operation with the U.S.A., this position might develop into an Anglo-Saxon hegemony. But was there really any likelihood that these hopes would be fulfilled? Hintze denied it with all the self-confidence of a man looking at the past from the watch-tower of a firm academic tradition. However often great empires might have been formed earlier in the history of the world, recent European history and its relationship with the most important factors in the world of his time seemed to him to be a sufficient guarantee that this could never happen again in the foreseeable future. The war showed even more clearly how deeply-rooted these ideas were in his mind. He repeated them in 1916 in the most prominent place possible, in the collection *Deutschland und der Weltkrieg*[1] which he published with Meinecke, Oncken, Schumacher and other eminent recent historians. The fact that Hintze was given the task both of introducing and concluding this representative collection reveals a great deal about the fundamental attitudes of the contributors. In his two essays Hintze gives an unadorned account of the course of German politics from 1900. He notes with obvious satisfaction that Germany had resisted the temptations of English diplomacy at the turn of the century and had not renounced her naval armament. He frankly admits that the English were quite right to deduce that German economic and maritime power might one day, if it continued to grow, jeopardize their own world supremacy. "This was in-

[1] Published in Berlin and Leipzig in 1916. He had already expressed similar ideas, in a less extreme, semi-official form, in his book on the Hohenzollern.

deed the essence of German policy. Our intention was to develop gradually in peaceful competition with England, until the older power would one day be forced to recognize us as an equal competitor in world politics. England is still far from granting any such equality to the continental powers, and the German refusal to admit England's sole supremacy at sea was certainly the main cause that drove the island kingdom into a war against Germany. Our aim in this war can only be to force England to abandon her claim to absolute supremacy at sea, and thus to create a state of equilibrium within the world system of states." England had always worked for such a balance within the European system, simply in order to control and regulate it from outside, while using this dazzling formula as a cover for her plans for world supremacy. Would she be able to carry out these plans in a war? Here again, Hintze is sufficiently sensitive to concede to the English that their dependence on sea communications made the struggle for absolute command of the seas a struggle for existence. He assesses the real motive power of England's resistance more soberly and profoundly than, for example, Delbrück. However, even in the middle of the bitter struggle, he still had confidence in an immanent trend in world history which, he thought, was running counter to the claims of the English. Like Tirpitz, he hoped that German naval armament would contribute to this trend. Our naval armament, he said, was quite clearly to the advantage of other sea-faring nations as well. "We hope that, sooner or later, other nations who are oppressed by the yoke of English supremacy at sea will also pluck up courage and decide to shake off their yoke. It is our aim to complement the balance of power on land with a balance of power at sea." This is Tirpitz's formulation word for word. "The effects of German naval armament are clearly making themselves felt in the peripheral territories of the Pacific. Japan is developing into a position of power, and we may soon hear the cry, 'Asia for the Asians'. The rise of Islam points in the same direction. The dream of a world governed by the white race is beginning to dissolve." We can see that, under the pressure of the war, Hintze was no longer afraid to unleash the Acheron of the coloured races. In fact he was finally informing our enemies that our nation had determined in its soul—as Frederick the Great had determined once before— that, if the worst came to the worst, we should bury ourselves and all our possessions beneath the ruins of European civilization rather than bow our heads beneath an enemy yoke.

But it is only occasionally that such alarming defiance breaks through. On the whole Hintze believes in the harmony of a future world balance of power and in the blessings that would spring from the vigorous co-existence of free peoples and states within a global framework, as previously within Europe. Germany, he said, was blazing the trail towards the freedom of all nations. She was exorcising the evil spirit that was threatening the world—the evil spirit of a final armed conflict between Russia and the Anglo-Saxons, and of a world state in whose Polypean embrace the civilization of the younger nations would inevitably be suffocated, as the civilizations of the ancient world had suffocated in the embrace of Rome.

When Hintze reaches the grand climax of his argument and quotes Geibel's words (quoted all too often at that time): "One day the world will be restored to health by the German spirit", we are well aware of the significance he attaches to them. In our counter-attack against the modern Rome, Napoleonic France, the German feeling of nationality had, for the first time, combined with that idea of individuality which had borne fruit a thousandfold in our spiritual life. Now Germany once again believed that she was being true to the best elements of her past by fighting the two world giants and so warding off the threat to national individuality. The idea that, in so doing, she was herself following in Napoleon's footsteps seemed to Hintze merely an absurd theory of English propagandists. Our situation, he said, was far more like that of Prussia in the Seven Years War. "What is at stake today is our ability to maintain ourselves among the world powers, just as what was at stake in the Seven Years War was our ability to maintain ourselves among the great powers of Europe." This comparison—at that time current coin among the educated—appealed most effectively to the determination of our encircled nation to assert itself. But was it really equal to the situation? Let us raise the question now; but before answering it, let us give a few more examples of the influence of the neo-Rankeans on interpretations of the situation in the world. In doing so, we cannot, of course, also hope to penetrate deeper into the individual views of the authors in question; it will be quite sufficient if we can show the spread—one is even tempted to say the universal presence—of certain typical ideas.

To find these ideas we need only turn, for example, to the work of Hermann Oncken. Himself a pupil of Max Lenz, he was a master in the art of illuminating the

broad patterns of foreign affairs. Speaking from the
most highly respected university chair in Germany,
and as the head of his own circle of pupils, he was able
to develop Ranke's ideas still further. That he was a
master in this art of illumination was proved by his
study on America and the Great Powers, dedicated
to Max Lenz, which appeared in 1900.[1] The subject,
America, takes him out beyond the circle of the great
European powers, whose history in the seventeenth
and eighteenth centuries had been the basis of Ranke's
view of the great powers. Although the stage for politics
on the grand scale had now grown until it included the
whole world, Oncken believed that the driving forces
were still the same as they had been on the previous,
more restricted stage. There can be no doubt that he
too subscribed to the idea that a world balance of power
would grow organically out of the older, narrower
system, as a tree grows out of a mustard seed; and that
this would be the completion of a development begun
long before, not a break in it. This becomes even more
apparent after the beginning of the war. At the end
of his work dealing with Central Europe, past and
present, which appeared in 1917, he raised his voice to
comfort Germany's small neighbours, saying that time
would tell which would be the greater threat to their
individuality: a proper balance of power in the world,
or the mere possibility of a balance of power in Europe
—which was anyway nothing more than a slogan
of English world expansionism. This world balance of
power was to be established, powerfully and systematically, by a German victory. The emphasis is exactly
the same as in Hintze's work. Moreover, between the

[1] Cf. Hermann Oncken, *Historisch-politische Aufsätze*, I, 3.

lines of the writings of both authors, we can read an admission that the days of the European balance of power, in the old sense of the term, would be numbered in the event of a German victory.[1]

We can sense basically similar ideas in the work of Erich Marcks—even at a very early date. In 1903 he wrote that the nations had simply overflowed the banks of their own countries into the world beyond, and that their imperialist strivings arose from their old underlying nationalism. This, he said, differentiated the imperialism of his time from the universal imperialism of Napoleon I and brought it closer to that of the national mercantile empires of the seventeenth and eighteenth centuries with their expansionist policies, and to the nationalist ideas of the nineteenth century. Marcks, too, goes on to justify the Wilhelminian navy, and the doctrine of risk underlying it, with the claim that the U.S.A. was clearly more dangerous to England's future than was Germany.[2] At the beginning of the war Marcks almost inevitably turned for enlightenment to Ranke's *Die grossen Mächte*. Once again he found the old antagonisms of the nineteenth century in the present; but, since the nationalist, people's states had become world states, the antagonisms had now grown to gigantic proportions. Germany, he said, wished to

---

[1] As far as I know, the historians we have studied never admitted that, at least in the European theatre, German politics had been forced into the Napoleonic path. Gustav Stresemann, who dared to do so, was, I think, a fairly isolated figure among the publicists.

[2] Cf. Erich Marcks's study of English foreign policy from 1500 to 1910 in *Männer und Zeiten*, II, p. 275. Marcks even thought that the first World War might be followed by a struggle between the two Anglo-Saxon empires for Canada and Australia. Cf. his *Englands Machtpolitik* (1940), p. 183.

become one of these world states; but England was perfectly free to remain one. It was only England's world supremacy that we did not recognize. With pathetic naïvety he regarded England's reply—war—as an unscrupulous and malevolent misinterpretation of our intentions. On this point Hintze's judgement was far more objective and sensitive. Nevertheless, the belief in a future concert of world powers, in the plurality of culture and power within the society of nations, and in Germany's duty to help to create this future by fighting England and her obsolete hegemony, was common to both men.

Meinecke also held this belief. In 1916 he republished Ranke's *Die grossen Mächte* with the Inselverlag, making it available to a large public; and in the same year, in the idealized plea for the German point of view that he contributed to *Deutschland und der Weltkrieg*, which we have already mentioned, he made an impressive appeal to the spirit of Ranke. "Our historical thinking and our cultural ideals are based on respect for the diversity and equality of strong and free states, nations and civilizations." The essential meaning of the events of recent European history, he went on, was that they led not to universal monarchy, as had previously been the case, but to vitality and wealth among powerful nations opposed to any attempt to establish a universal monarchy. "Universal maritime supremacy is only another form of universal monarchy, which cannot be tolerated and must, sooner or later, fail. England is fighting against the spirit of modern development. . . . Her significance as a world nation and a world civilization, which we recognize, will not suffer if the balance of power, which she has tried in the past to restrict artificially within the limits of Europe, is extended to include the oceans and the world beyond. Only then will every nation have the free breathing-space it requires." This picture of the future by a great exponent of the History of Ideas is, like his own nature, bright and harmonious. But does it face the facts? Hintze had seen more clearly the repercussions on the island power of a breakdown of its supremacy at sea, while Oncken had hinted at the possible repercussions on the European balance of power. But Meinecke, less a devotee of power than any of his friends, could not come to terms with the brutal laws of power conflicts, and so, later, never ceased to hope for a negotiated peace once it had become clear that English sea power could not be destroyed.

We can understand how gratefully these German historians welcomed *Die Grossmächte der Gegenwart* by the Swedish historian Kjellen, for it was an echo confirming all their dearest personal beliefs. This work, which appeared just before the war, expressed German hopes more frankly than the Germans could decently have done themselves. It was no coincidence that the title was reminiscent of Ranke's essay which we have so often cited. Ranke's basic idea of the individuality and vital function of the great powers became flesh and blood in Kjellen's word. He consistently denied that the future could bring universalism, offering a multitude of reasons. In particular, England's supremacy at sea seemed to him only to conform to a situation that world history would certainly eradicate. Just as the balance of power had established itself on land after 1500, so it would now at sea. Even the united and victorious power of the Anglo-Saxons would not be able to prevent this, for the attempt would instantly evoke an opposing coalition, and the same would occur in the event of a Russian victory. Once again, experience in Europe was applied uncritically to a consideration of the situation in the world outside Europe. Kjellen even thought—and, as a citizen of a small state, thought with obvious satisfaction—that even if, within the system, our age had produced a world of large estates, the general political development might still lead back to small-holding. Max Lenz had already deduced this development from Ranke's premises, and it had often been prophesied by other Rankeans since.

Lenz, Delbrück, Hintze, Marcks, Meinecke—to continue this line to the *dii minores* would only weary the reader. The situation was exactly as Walter Vogel summarized it so pregnantly when he looked back on it after the war. "Before 1914, German observers were generally agreed that it must be Germany's task in history to transform the balance of power in Europe into a balance embracing the whole world."[1] It could justifiably be said that this interpretation was the banner under which the majority of our historians marched, credulously and in close formation, from the turn of the century until the end of the war.

But in spite of our initial successes, the World War brought this march to a halt. The terrible reality it disclosed was quite different from the prospect that had always been described. The great surge of the old European melody drowned the timid world tune that we thought we had heard.

Rational thinking therefore had to give place to

[1] Walter Vogel, *Das neue Europa* (1921), p. 51.

60

intellectual improvisation. But if we had not been able to agree on any national plans under a rising star, how were we ever to agree on improvisations under a setting one? Some wanted to retreat a little way and extract from the unexpected horror a negotiated peace that would preserve the possibility of fresh advance.[1] Others became keener than ever to force their way past the unforeseen obstacles and march to a victorious peace. Both groups had illusions of one kind or another about the resources that the English could summon in defence of their insular security; but the champions of a victorious peace had by far the more dangerous illusions, for the more they lost at the game, the more they raised their stakes. In their historical thinking both groups, disappointed in their world-wide speculations, tended more and more to retreat blindly into the shelter afforded by the history of their own nation; for it is a legitimate reaction for a nation faced with urgent difficulties to turn for support to the memory of earlier difficulties successfully overcome. The Seven Years War, which had been a war of encirclement, now proved an invaluable comfort to the encircled nation. Whether or not it contained any objective lessons besides its subjective encouragement was, of course, another question altogether. The advocates of negotiation

---

[1] Delbrück, the main spokesman for a negotiated peace, expressed a secret hope in 1916 that England's power would disintegrate from within after the war. Cf. *Krieg und Politik*, I, p. 243. Moreover, in May 1918 he was still demanding for Germany the following "essential" conditions for a negotiated peace: freedom of the seas, and a colonial empire that would assure us the position of a world power. He added that there could be no hope of peace while Lloyd George remained in power. Cf. the leaflet *Englands Schuld am Kriege*.

in particular believed that it was a model and that, by copying it, they could achieve a successful defensive policy that would wear down the enemy and guarantee the position and future of the state, even if its frontiers could not be extended. However, even the comparison with the Seven Years War involved a risk of reaching false conclusions, though these false conclusions were different from those inherent in the comparison with the whole of world history. The latter tended to draw attention too far away from the natural home of our power and into the sphere of the oceans, while the former were too closely tied to obsolete continental traditions—in two senses. First, while it was true to say that Prussia had merely maintained her territory in the Seven Years War, the war had also confirmed her acquisition of Silesia and her previously established position as a great power. But merely to maintain herself within her own frontiers in the World War would not have helped to establish Germany's position as a world power, for she was still engaged in trying to achieve that position. Secondly, the Seven Years War was a continental war waged by three continental powers against a fourth. It was indeed associated with a war at sea, but the war at sea was directed against France, not against Prussia; on the contrary, it brought Prussia her alliance with the English. Ranke's famous, but rhetorically exaggerated, words—that Prussia had shown herself to be a great power in 1763 because she had stood firm "against everybody else" and against "all the rest of Europe"—were often repeated in Germany, and these and similar phrases tempted us to regard the Seven Years War as a genuine forerunner of the World War. Yet on the

most important point there could be no question of
similarity, for our relationship with England at that
time had been the exact opposite of what it was now.
Only a comparison with one of the three earlier
struggles for hegemony could have offered a sufficient,
or a really instructive, parallel; but this was the very
comparison that, half unconsciously, we avoided, because it would inevitably have shattered our confidence, not strengthened it.

Not even the invocation of the spirit of Frederick the
Great could postpone the catastrophe. Our hopes that
our national history would prove to have some continuity—hopes which had been raised too high—and
our hopes that world history (which we had misunderstood) would display some similar continuity disappeared into the chaos. Could the academic historians
build a more solid structure to replace their older
buildings, which now stood in ruins? Could they
intellectually master the overwhelming impact of
recent events and turn it into genuine experience?
Could they add this to the mass of learning gradually
built up over the previous hundred years and make the
whole into a unity as impressive as that which had,
after all, existed until 1914? It would inevitably depend on the answer to this question, whether or not
historiography would be able to maintain its important
position in the life of the nation, in spite of the undermining of its authority by the reverse suffered by it
and so many other authoritative spheres of life, and in
spite of the spreading disintegration of the bourgeois
world. We cannot, within the limited framework of
our particular subject, venture on a discussion of this
great problem, which has faced us again, with terrible

gravity, since 1945. It will be sufficient if we can contribute an aphoristic epilogue to the discussion by following something of the last stages and the dissolution of neo-Rankeanism.

The move away from pre-war ideas can perhaps be seen most impressively in Meinecke's essay, published in 1919, where he spoke of the parallels to our situation to be found in the history of the world.[1] With valiant and elastic independence of mind he firmly faced the unexpected possibility that the lessons of modern European history might have lost their validity and that the old tendency towards a balance of power might have given place to a new tendency towards world supremacy. The memory of the *imperium Romanum* inevitably emerged from the mists of what had been supposed to be distant history— awakened purely by power politics, just as it had been awakened several decades before, in Jakob Burckhardt's speculations, by cultural events. How had events come to take this unexpected turn? Meinecke did not think it had been inevitable: but then he was one of those who had hoped for a Hubertusburg peace.[2] After the opportunity for agreement had been missed he saw the evil spirit of the *imperium Anglo-Saxonicum* looming over the horizon—but now, he said, the old tendency to split into nationalities no longer had the strength to dispel it. He soberly recognized the dynamic, unifying nature of modern civilization, especially in the form of world economics, and he saw

[1] Cf. Friederich Meinecke, *Nach der Revolution.*

[2] Translator's Note. Hubertusburg was the castle where peace was signed on 15 February 1763 at the end of the Seven Years War.

64

that, if directed by the two Anglo-Saxon empires and given the military support of their navies, this civilization might have the power permanently to suppress the autonomy of nations. Just as he compared the Anglo-Saxons with the Romans, so he compared the nation states on the continent with the Greek *poleis*. He clearly heralded the concept of a cultural empire standing like a vault over the old and smaller system of civilized states; and by making the retrospective comparison with Greece instead of the more usual one with modern European history, he graphically illustrated the complete reversal of his earlier diagnosis. Thus he greatly extended his horizon and discovered parallels that even Ranke never drew in his studies of world history. Jakob Burckhardt's star was in the ascendant.

But the way towards a radical reassessment of our view of political history opened up by this prophetic essay was scarcely explored any further. It was too unfamiliar and it involved a renunciation too great for our selfish feelings;[1] moreover, it was soon discredited by the retreat of the U.S.A. into isolation. Meinecke himself, however, gave expression to his changed feelings in another place—perhaps that dearest to him: in his book *Die Idee der Staatsräson*.

In the years following Versailles the attention of political historians was devoted entirely to a semipolitical task concerned with the present—the rectification of the one-sided theory of war guilt contained in the treaty. This was a rewarding task, but not

[1] Hermann Oncken, in *Nation und Geschichte* (1924), p. 42, said: "The history of the last thousand years shows that we have not been called upon to play the role of the Greeks in the world, nor yet that of the Jews."

without its special dangers; for in an atmosphere of national self-justification, it is all too easy to lose that uninhibited impartiality which is essential if depressing happenings are to be transformed into genuine experience. This transformation could not be achieved simply by producing documentary proof, however irrefutable, to exonerate Germany from the charge of having prepared the conflagration. What was needed was a really profound examination of the role played by our rigid concepts of politics in changing the whole diplomatic climate, an examination of the significance to be attached to public opinion in our country, and finally, an examination of the prospects presented by Germany's general political and geographical situation. It was naturally very difficult for men who had been spokesmen of official opinion—in the governmental sense in which the term was used before 1914—to make such an examination. But the main deterrent against impartial introspection was the partly justified fear of giving the enemy new material for indictments; and this obstacle even affected our understanding of the war itself. While our enemies' propaganda had never ceased to accuse us of deliberately adopting Napoleonic policies, we on our side were unwilling to admit that our struggle against the coalition opposed to us had quite logically given to the war the familiar form of earlier struggles for hegemony. Yet without this admission there could be no deeper and more penetrating understanding of the war—even of the military events alone, not to speak of the political problems, which began with our need for future security and proceeded inevitably to thoughts of hegemony, however we might formulate them.

It was not only the question of war guilt that diverted our historical thinking from its principal task. There was a second task concerned with the present—also a semi-political one and also defensive in nature—which had a similar effect: the task of building moral defences against France's belated and paradoxical supremacy after 1919. Faced with the withdrawal of Russia and the United States—the two powers who were to decide the future—we narrowed our horizon almost to the point where it embraced no more than the politics of the *ancien régime*; and the picture that Ranke had originally drawn of the great powers—even without any projection on to the world outside Europe —thus assumed a new immediacy. There began a renaissance of the old form of Rankeanism (if I may be allowed the expression) and a resurgence of feelings and ideas dating from days long past, when France was still the dominating power, the hereditary enemy overshadowing the whole of Europe and especially her German neighbour.

But, influenced by our opposition to France, we were all too easily led astray by analogies between previous centuries and the present, just as earlier we had been similarly led astray under the influence of our opposition to England; for a comparison between the France of Poincaré and the France of Louis XIV or Napoleon I was devoid of all substance. France's inner strength no longer corresponded to her armed force, nor did Europe play the same role in the world as before. Up to a point the comparison might give valid results; but to use it as the basis for an evaluation of the entire political situation was to conjure up illusions. To emphasize only a single vital point: England's differences with France were by no means the fundamental factor underlying her policy, as they had been in previous centuries. She now regarded France as an extremely awkward ally, not as a serious rival. It was a forlorn hope for Erich Marcks, Brandenberg and others to demand that England should form a grand coalition against France analogous to the grand coalitions formed against Napoleon and Louis XIV.

Such attempts to reach an historical understanding of the present remained entirely shackled by desires and habits. They never attained to the cool clarity that distinguishes Meinecke's sketch. Moreover, they concerned themselves only with the continent: the world beyond was not considered.

It is not surprising, then, that when their hopes revived, the Germans should have returned to the concept of a world system of states. There are obvious signs of this in Marcks's writings; but even among the younger generation of historians there were some who began to revert to old ways of thinking. Let us quote two striking examples. A. Rein concluded an instructive essay on the significance of overseas expansion to the European system[1] with a projection of "traditional conditions in the West" on to "the sphere of the combined political forces of the whole world" (and how well we know this projection by now). He wanted to see the Great War as a stage on the road from the old European system to a new world system. His idea was to develop a theory for the new world system, similar to the many tentative theories, historical and theoretical, put forward for a European system in the eighteenth century. Almost inevitably this general

[1] *Historische Zeitschrift*, Vol. 137 (1928).

view of the subject was again combined with a specific hope—the hope that the British Empire would disintegrate. "It may be that a genuine world system of states cannot develop until a later date, when the unique, world-wide political link of the British *imperium* has been completely severed." The *fata morgana* has still not touched firm ground; it hovers above the earth, diametrically opposed to the *imperium Anglo-Saxonicum.*

Almost at the same time Wolfgang Windelband's book *Die auswärtige Politik der Grossmächte in der Neuzeit (1491–1919)*, published in 1922, which went into several editions, revived some of Ranke's ideas with special emphasis. Once again these ideas were projected on to the world outside Europe. In the introduction Windelband says straight away that the system of states, which at first included only the Germanic and Roman peoples, extended northwards and eastwards to form the European system, and that it will reach its final fulfilment in a world system of states. At the end of the book we even have a reappearance of Delbrück's theory that England's position in the world at large corresponded to the position that Napoleon occupied in Europe. But Windelband left unanswered the question of why, in the World War, events should suddenly have escaped from their well-worn, centuries-old rut and helped the power wielding hegemony, not the system of states to victory. Ultimately the reader still has to turn for consolation to a world system of states, which will finally be established and will offer Germany opportunities for resurgence. The experience gained in the World War, which pointed in the opposite direction, was more or less ignored.

This is the depressing general impression left by even the briefest study of the post-war period. In contrast to the enormous mass of publications on the crisis, there were no real works of synthesis—not even in the sphere of military events, where a general survey should have been easiest. Events at sea and on land were nearly always treated separately; they were not co-ordinated to form any wider, comprehensive picture. This made it all the easier for the instinctive continental mentality—the soil in which the legend of the stab in the back and every other kind of misunderstanding was to grow—to assert itself. I believe that these misunderstandings were connected with our national fear of using the one key that would most surely have opened the locked door—our fear of using the morphological relationship between the various European crises in modern history to help us to understand the crisis that had just occurred. I need hardly add that we should have needed the ability to recognize not only typical phenomena, but particular phenomena as well. In other words, our greatest need would have been some insight into the much greater threat to our whole moral and material existence inherent in a war for supremacy fought in the climate, so pregnant with disaster, of modern global civilization.

Be that as it may, our historians were not able in the short time at their disposal to produce a convincing interpretation of the first World War, firmly grounded in a comprehensive historical panorama and therefore immune to both national sensibilities and political interests. They failed to solve the problem nearest home, which was infinitely the hardest problem to solve. It was the problem of distilling out of the bloody massacre some precious experience to serve as a medicine against a relapse into impulsive blindness. But to what extent could such experience have been effective? That is a question that should not be asked by anyone speaking in this age of reason. *Periculum in mora*—even today.

THOUGHTS ON GERMANY'S
MISSION 1900–1918

IN his first major work[1] Friederich Meinecke
advanced the idea of the German nation state as a
development from the concept of world citizenship.
He did so, at that time, in the confident belief that this
idea had found its lasting fulfilment in Bismarck's
Reich. However, in the very years which saw the
formation of the ideas embodied in this epoch-making
book, the Reich was developing further and further
towards the imperialism which, unexpectedly, was
once more to jeopardize the political forms that had
been successfully established.[2] The first World War,
the paradoxical outcome of our entry into world affairs,
forced us into a struggle on our own doorstep—the
struggle for European hegemony. In doing so, it
threatened not only the very existence of our state, but
also its inner character as a nation state. Germany, last
among her neighbours in Europe, had only just and
with great difficulty succeeded in crystallizing this
national character. Thus it was that during the war
Meinecke began to criticize more and more sharply the
exaggerations and distortions that he saw around him.
As he himself said, he began to retrace the steps he had

[1] *Weltbürgertum und Nationalstaat*, 1st ed. (1908).
[2] Perhaps the most striking evidence of this can be found in
Friedrich Naumann's *National-sozialer Katechismus*, published in
1897. There he writes: "What is nationalism? It is the urge of the
German people to spread its influence all over the globe."

taken in his book—that is, to move towards the concept of world citizenship which had been his point of departure. His ideas began to change and to undergo the great development that was to give him the necessary strength for his spiritual resistance in the second phase of our fanatical drive towards hegemony after 1933. Let us now try to add an epilogue, as it were, to the great man's work and to discuss the intensification of imperialism within the idea of the nation state after 1900, and then of its first distortion into a drive for hegemony after 1914.

The idea of a nation state *within* Europe, as it had crystallized in the course of the nineteenth century, and that of supremacy *over* Europe are in conflict with one another. The first presumes that a nation state will take its place within a group of similar states with equal rights, while the second sees a single state set up over all the rest. This is a contrast which allows of transitions from one possibility to the other; for a supreme power can in fact accentuate and enhance its own national character only by using its supremacy to subdue this very character in other states. This condition might be described as hypertrophy of one nation state at the expense of others.

In the course of the last few decades Germany has hurried through this whole development, from a limited, purely national existence to an attempt to achieve hegemony. Let us try to select a few examples to illustrate this development from the turn of the century until after the beginning of the first World War, drawing especially on the imperialism tinged with liberalism which most significantly represented the growing, vigorous, expansionist self-confidence of the time and to which Meinecke himself to some extent subscribed. Even if, in terms of numbers, it did not command a very wide following, this imperialism did embrace those who supplied the influential middle voices within the polyphonic choir of public opinion— the voices that were heeded in, and sometimes even conducted from, government offices. We have long felt it to be an urgent task not only to explain the particular actions of governments in voluminous publications of documents, but also to understand the attitude of those whom they governed and whose approval or criticism helped to shape those documents. How can one hope to understand the movements of a ship if one fails to take into account the wind and the waves?

As soon as we apply ourselves to this task, we feel restrained by the emotional inhibitions connected with the question of war guilt, which still obscure our view as powder-smoke may blur contours after a battle. These inhibitions cannot greatly affect the description of diplomatic actions, for these were the actions that gave rise to the most telling arguments against the one-sided, anti-German theory of war-guilt which we felt to be expressed in the Treaty of Versailles. Yet this powder-smoke becomes more dangerous should we wish to evaluate the complex dynamism of the German people as a whole, which certainly in some sense underlay these governmental actions. The works which appeared in the twenties and thirties, and which are still authoritative, have not done justice to this dynamism; nor has the second World War left an atmosphere in which it is easier for us Germans to rectify this omission, in spite of the fact that the similarities between the course of the two World Wars, as also the lapse of time since 1914, should both serve to make intelligent and fruitful re-appraisal easier.

(a)

As his contribution to the controversy surrounding the beginning of the Seven Years War, Thomas Mann remarks, as though this were the war guilt question of the eighteenth century, that at bottom the younger and more ambitious state is always the aggressor. This observation, taken in its broadest sense, may serve as our point of departure, for it is certainly true that it is inherent in the nature of the younger and more ambitious state, sometimes instinctively, sometimes deliberately, to try to win territory from the older *beati possidentes*. But if the younger state has such immense forces of elemental civilization at its command as had the Wilhelminian Reich (in contrast to those behind the earlier and artificial Prussian efforts at expansion), then its neighbours, who have no similar vitality to oppose it, must inevitably suspect it of disrupting the peace. This is especially true if, like Germany, it moves into a new sphere of activity, the ocean, where it has no previous experience on which to draw as a moderating influence, and in which it threatens to affect the entire *status quo* of the system of states. Thus it is futile to cite general phenomena side by side with Germany's individual dynamism and to be content with the colourless conclusion that, in one way or another, all the great powers contributed to the catastrophe. This view is perfectly admissible in a specific investigation of war guilt or *culpa*; but it cannot satisfy those who are searching for the deeper roots of events, the *causa*.

This particular dynamism is the powerful force underlying Germany's "peaceful" policies, and more particularly their nucleus, her naval armament. From it German armament derives its special character, which cannot be expressed in the simple alternative between war and peace but rather demands a more elastic, neutral term, oscillating between the two poles of war and peace. The term "Cold War", to which our daily experience has today given so much meaning, is such a term. Should we reject it as an anachronism? Surely it simply serves to make us aware of the similarity between the tensions existing then and now, even if today's tensions are similar only in kind, not in degree. An even better reason for using the term is that a closely related term, the "Dry War", which Delbrück sometimes applied to the Anglo-German arms race, had already been coined at the time.[1]

What are the characteristics of such a "dry" or "cold" war? The ultimate ambition of those who wage it is to achieve their aims peacefully. But these aims are offensive and not defensive. The intention is to force the opponent out of his present position and rank, and achieve what can otherwise be achieved only by the use of arms. Arms, too, play their part; for in order to impose the desired course, whether by fear or by threats, the production of arms is accelerated— always in the hope that it will not be necessary to have recourse to them. The whole idea is that one's own

[1] *Preussische Jahrbücher* (November 1910), p. 266. Widenmann, in his memoirs, *Marineattaché in London 1907–12* (1952), p. 312, used the term "latent war".

arms should so increase the risk of war that one's opponent will not dare to break from the cold war forced upon him into a hot one, and that, exhausted, he will cede his position peacefully. But is it ever safe to count on such a peaceful surrender? Surely not. A peaceful offensive of this kind must itself also accept a risk of war, the only difference being that the decision to strike the first blow can, if necessary, be forced upon the other side. In this way the roles of aggressor and defender can, in the undesirable event of actual war, seem to have been completely reversed. In general terms the whole development that we have discussed always displays a blend of offensive and defensive elements and of peaceful and belligerent ones, but in such proportions that, in fact, the peaceful offensive ambitions of the rising power dominate the scene until the critical moment when the goaded opponent may risk the final step into war.

Those who can project themselves into the perpetually shifting dialectic of a cold war will recognize that a cold war was going on even at those times in the Wilhelminian period when the changes in policy of a divided political leadership were even more frequent than the changeable nature of a cold war demands. Moreover, we must never forget that it was the central element in the German programme—her naval armament—which proved decisive.

German policy did not of course rely solely on the forced development of the country's military potential. It also calculated on the growth of the economy and the population and regarded both as of primary importance. However, economic and demographic growth upheld and promoted military strength; and so, in the last analysis it was naval armament which determined our fate.

The writings of the publicists show the intellectual and emotional background to this programme of armament less inhibitedly and more comprehensively than official files, which are split up into isolated topics. The files show us the trees, but the publicists make us aware of the wood.

It is immediately obvious that, in spite of the familiar defensive arguments thrust into the foreground—and what nation engaged in armament does not exploit such arguments?—our naval armament was ultimately intended, from the very first, to achieve a great offensive aim. It was, as far as possible, to cater for the peaceful achievement of this aim, but at the same time to cover the danger of war. What was this ultimate aim?

It was not the realization of any particular territorial gain anywhere in the world, though there was no lack of extravagant individual desires for expansion. In this respect, therefore, the aim may seem blurred and imprecise.[1] In fact it consisted of both more and less than this. It consisted in securing a new outlet for Germany's power through her navy, and in achieving equality, both in prestige and in actual fact, with the other world powers in the coming world system of states. But, expressed in another way, this meant that it consisted in the expulsion of England from her posi-

[1] P. Rohrbach, in *Der deutsche Gedanke in der Welt* (1912), p. 202, wrote: "However, the main reason why our position sometimes makes such an uncertain, even unpleasant, impression when seen from outside Germany lies in the difficulty of presenting any easily comprehensible, as it were tangible, aim for the policies demanded by German ideas."

tion of supremacy, for it was this supremacy that stood in the way of the formation of a really free world system of states.[1] Territorial gains or, as Friedrich Naumann called them, "great incursions into the history of the world",[2] would follow of their own accord.

It follows that there was no question of our using maritime supremacy to defend what we had; we were enlisting its help to win peacefully what we wanted— the position of a world power. This offensive aim alone can sufficiently explain our naval armament, and it was formulated again and again after the turn of the century. Delbrück repeatedly and quite openly wrote that the tension between Germany and England was not a product of commercial rivalry, the interpretation to which both popular and official opinion clung. Indeed our navy was not intended to protect our commerce, but—and I think that we are justified in summarizing his opinion in these words—to produce a change in the power relationships of the world to Germany's advantage; to establish a global balance of power at sea like the European balance of power on land; and to eliminate English maritime supremacy, as Napoleon's supremacy on land had been destroyed. Thus it fulfilled what was essentially an offensive not a defensive function—though the second is of course contained within the first. As we seemed to progress towards the fulfilment of this task, Delbrück believed that he was already in a position to make continual

[1] P. Rohrbach, *op. cit.*, p. 191: "If fate should have decided that we are not to achieve our aim of becoming a world power, the decision must be announced, not by the proclamation of English supremacy, but in the language of guns." Cf. also the essay on *Ranke and German Imperialism*, above.

[2] W. Conze in *Kaehler Festschrift*, p. 365.

demands on England, even if only at the expense of third parties.[1] For he was aware that the German navy made the Reich a greater danger to the island kingdom than to any other state and that maritime power is by its very nature more vulnerable than land power. England's very existence depended on maritime supremacy: were she to suffer a defeat at sea, she would never be able to recover. Of course, Delbrück assured the English that we only intended to eliminate their *universal* power and that we had no intention of going any further—in other words, that we should allow her to remain a world power *alongside* other powers.[2] But could this naïve assurance, which sprang from Delbrück's fear that Germany might drift into the Napoleonic road to hegemony, hope to reassure an Englishman even if it were honest? Surely not, for the loss of her universal supremacy would make the island dependent on the goodwill of her continental rival.

If we find such evidence in the writings of the publicists of the offensive aims of our policies—and it would be easy to cite more[3]—we may perhaps ask to what extent the antagonism between England and Germany, and so, ultimately, the explosion of 1914, should be blamed on "misunderstandings". In the oppressive, nervous atmosphere of those years there

[1] H. Delbrück, in *Vor und nach dem Weltkrieg* (Berlin, 1926), p. 370 (written in 1912), said that the navy was not developed to protect commerce, but to win "a just share of world power". For Delbrück's ideas on foreign policy, cf. also *Ranke and German Imperialism*, above, and A. Steger's Marburg thesis on Delbrück (1955).

[2] Cf. *Preussische Jahrbücher* (October 1906).

[3] *Ranke and German Imperialism*, above. In this connection, cf. also the ideas of Friedrich Naumann, Rohrbach and Max Weber.

were certainly plenty of misunderstandings, both intentional and unintentional, on both sides. But these misunderstandings were not the decisive factor; they were merely the shell round a hard core of diametrically opposed vital interests, like the aureole of light round the moon on a damp night.

On the English side Sir Eyre Crowe, for example, in his notorious memorandum of New Year's Day 1907, misunderstood many of Germany's ideas,[1] quite apart from his hateful misinterpretation of diplomatic events. But did he not for all that have a clear vision of the main problem, the danger threatening England? For even if Germany were not consciously aiming at hegemony, the world balance of power for which she was working involved the destruction of English maritime supremacy and thus a threat to English existence. This was quite sufficient to alarm England. "This is not the matter in which England can safely run any risk."

On the German side England's intentions were largely misunderstood, and were painted in dark colours because we instinctively wanted to see them in this way in order to justify our own intentions. The essential point, however, was the nature of these intentions. They tended towards a cold offensive; thus, in accordance with the laws of cold war, they inevitably accepted the risk of hot war.

The spokesmen for public opnion whom we are considering were certainly aware of this risk from the outset. In periods of confidence, such as the first few

[1] Crowe also misunderstood Delbrück, believing, strangely enough, that he was more harmless than he really was. Cf. *British Documents on the Origins of the War*, Vol. III, p. 414.

years of the century, when the diplomatic situation favoured Germany, they bore the risk lightly. In succeeding periods of anxiety, as the diplomatic situation turned against Germany, they bore it with fatalistic defiance. In neither case, however, did any of them contemplate renouncing the ultimate offensive aim, in spite of the great differences of temperament between them.

Let us consider a few examples. In 1896, when the idea of the new navy was still being hatched, Friedrich Naumann maintained that colonies for settlers could be won only after victory at sea. Even at this time the possibility of a real war did not apparently lie beyond the bounds of his imagination, and even though later he joined the cold war faction, this idea is none the less a particularly recurrent one in his writings. Again and again a trial of strength with England in a "world war" seemed to him inevitable.[1] However, the world war that Naumann imagined at the turn of the century was exactly the opposite of the one that finally took place. "If there is anything certain in the history of the world," he wrote in 1900, "it is the future outbreak of a world war, i.e. a war fought by those who seek to deliver themselves from England." Here, surely, we have the German miscalculation expressed with epigrammatic brevity. In 1900 Max Lenz, a historian, coined his rousing slogan about a future War of the English Succession and thereby threw into sharp relief

---

[1] W. Conze, *loc. cit.*, pp. 363, 365. Cf. also R. Nürnberger on Naumann in *Historische Zeitschrift*, Vol. 170, 3, p. 530, where he publishes the following quotation, dating from 1895: "To be anything at all, one must have an ambition to win something in the world."

our militant willingness to act in the event of "a redistribution of the World" (Bülow), if necessary by force of arms. In 1902, after the beginning of the cold war, even Lenz's more cautious friend Delbrück was prepared openly to threaten a hot one. If England would not cede her maritime supremacy peacefully, he said, she might be struck down by the same fate as Napoleon III, who had refused to give up France's claims to hegemony on land.[1] Later, of course, during the lean years of encirclement, his great fear was of a hot war in Europe which might force Germany to embark upon Napoleon I's fatal course. Until 1914 he hoped optimistically for a continuation of the cold war, and then, until 1918, at least for peace by agreement; but he never considered the possibility of renouncing the ultimate aim in world politics, and he was prepared to face any risk in order to keep open the road to its fulfilment. Max Weber, on the other hand, was positively defiant in his recognition of the inevitable risk of war inherent in Germany's rise. Looking back in 1916 he exclaimed: "Had we not been prepared to risk this war, then we should never have bothered to found the Reich."[2] But as early as 1895, in his inaugural lecture, he had thundered forth his great imperialistic pronouncement—which was enthusiastically adopted —that the foundation of the Reich would have been as pointless as a childish prank, had not a superstructure of world politics been built upon it. P. Rohrbach felt himself similarly drawn into accepting the risk of war

[1] Delbrück, *Vor und nach dem Weltkriege* (Berlin, 1926), p. 58.
[2] Lecture of 22 October 1916, printed in Max Weber's collected political writings. In the same collection, cf. also his inaugural lecture.

by the dynamic rise, so rich in promise, of Prussia and Germany. He too saw the significance of the foundation of the Reich in the fact that it had enabled us to compete with England at the eleventh hour. He made his attitude to this competition clear when he said that if England would not cede her supremacy voluntarily, then guns must speak. He was, however, magnanimous enough to add that we should have no cause for complaint if, in such a position, England preferred to fight rather than give in.[1]

There can be no doubt that, especially in the last years before the outbreak of the war, the liberal imperialists, and with them wide circles of the upper classes, were prepared to accept the risk of a European war rather than renounce the ultimate offensive aim which they had set themselves at the turn of the century. Needless to say, their willingness in no way represented an active desire nor, to the very last, did it rule out the possibility of abrupt changes of policy, be they colonial agreements or a temporary redirection of the pressure of the armament programme from the navy to the army. But these changes of policy were never intended to be interpreted as a renunciation of the naval arms race: on the contrary, they were merely intended in some measure to parry English countermoves on the continent. The great aim remained unchanged: to force England out of her position of supremacy.

Naturally the narrower the navigable channel of the cold war became, the more our *sang-froid* deserted us and the more nervously did this willingness to under-

---

[1] P. Rohrbach, *Der deutsche Gedanke in der Welt* (1912), p. 190. On Rohrbach, cf. Maibaum's Marburg thesis (1955).

take even the ultimate step find expression in sabre-rattling and even in our toying with the idea of a preventive war. The reviving importance of the Pan-Germans provided a barometer for this atmosphere. This revival could not be deduced from their meagre following but, in spite of their small numbers, their ideas suddenly spread more and more quickly. It is the crests that show the height of the waves beneath. Although foreign observers often overestimated the power of the Pan-German League in specific cases, their suspicions later proved to have been, on the whole, too modest. Though they may have exaggerated the influence of the Pan-Germans in the Foreign Ministry, this influence was indisputably at work in the Admiralty, whose chief, and not the Imperial Chancellor, was the man of destiny in the years before the war.

(b)

We have now unwittingly reached the threshold between the cold war and the hot. But we must not cross it without asking the authors upon whom we have drawn the question which mainly interests us. What ideal was to be served by the drive for power that we have observed? What mission, beyond purely national interests, were they furthering when they advocated this drive?

It must be stressed at once that at this period every country was clearly characterized by the predominance of policies of absolute self-interest, which narrowed the scope of intellectual forces more severely than in previous generations. This was especially true of that impetuous late-comer, the second Prussian Reich, and it was characteristic that our imperialist historians should have been so eager to draw parallels between the ambitions of their time and the sober, cautious mercantilism of the eighteenth century.[1]

Nevertheless, the bright ideal of the political self-assertion of individual nations within a circle of equals gave even German imperialism a thin, glittering veneer of intellectualism which the calculating mercantilism of the *ancien régime* had never had. This ideal had evolved later in our minds than elsewhere in the West; with us it could not consequently penetrate so deeply into the lower layers of the European spirit nor combine so closely with universal and normative elements, with Natural Law and Christianity; but it did find a place within a wider view of the world which sought God in the specific not in the general, in existence not in obligation—a system which saw no cause for alarm in the multitude of rival historic nations nor in the chaos which these involved, but throve on it and prized it as a thing of value, filled with a mysterious harmony. So we always saw the European system of states, which had been the prerequisite for our rise in the nineteenth century, surrounded by a nimbus of ideals. This explains why our imperialists so unsuspectingly applied this interpretation, which had proved itself so well in Europe, to conditions in the world at large. We expected to find a free world system of states offering a position of equality for Germany. We felt that our imperialism was not a completely new factor, but rather an organic continuation of what had gone

---

[1] Otto Hintze did so with particular weight and emphasis; but the idea had a wide following.

before. That is why even the younger generation, however realistic their thought, still turned confidently towards the classical period of our spiritual history, especially as certain aspects of this period, above all certain aspects of Hegel's philosophy[1] and of Ranke's historiography, could provide such an excellent justification of modern practice. Was it not true to say that the political tasks facing the two periods were, in some respects, essentially similar? Did not our ancestors' fight against French hegemony on land resemble our own against English hegemony at sea? Was it not certain that the spiritual individuality of the nations of the world must one day triumph over the Grand Fleet, as it had over the Grand Army? Of course this meant that, in building up her own fleet, Germany was not only recognizing her own interests, but was at the same time fulfilling her mission to the world. She was representing a great ideal of justice for all nations—the ideal that civilization should develop only through the diversity of free nations all over the world. Ultimate success must of necessity fall to Germany,[2] for hers was the role of Hegel's world spirit.

In arguing in this way our liberal imperialists in particular were seeking a weapon against the successful

[1] Heller, *Hegel und der nationale Machtstaatsgedanke* (1921).

[2] The following are some of the varied and widely accepted ideas that Hans Delbrück publicized as early as 1899, in *Preussische Jahrbücher* (February 1899): the spread of the German way of life would benefit not only the German people, but the whole of humanity; for the sake of humanity as a whole, Germany must ensure that a certain balance of power existed between the great nations and the small, in the world outside Europe; the spiritual wealth of our age lay in the peaceful existence, side by side, of civilized nations following their own particular development—and so on.

competition of the older Western states, which they so much feared.[1] While they were trying to find some specifically and exclusively German idea of freedom promising independence to the weak and oppressed nations, as a reply to the more current Western idea, they were also undermining the great empires which were keeping Germany in the shade. The policies dictated by our material interests went hand in hand with our bright ideals. One might almost say that in this sphere, as in so many others, Germany was learning from her English rivals, preparing for herself a role in world poiitics basically similar to that played for centuries by England in European politics—the role of champion of a diversity of free states against hegemony, of the weak against the strong. We saw the ever-growing giants of hegemony, England and Russia, overshadowing the world. The task that we had undertaken was not only to win a place in the sun for ourselves, but also to assure a brighter existence for others—for the Egyptians and the Persians, the whole of Islam and the Indians, the Boers and the Indo-Chinese, the Chinese and the Latin Americans.

Of course this concern for those in the shade might well have hidden a certain degree of hypocrisy: "Small states are promised freedom so that they shall change their masters" (Friedrich Naumann).[2] But to

[1] P. Rohrbach, *loc. cit.*, p. 217. Here there is already a treatment of the problem of Germany's unpopularity in the world—which also occupied Delbrück and was later taken up by Max Scheler. The most intelligent analyses of the German idea of freedom, as against the Western idea, were given in the war years by Meinecke and Troeltsch. However, these analyses are only a development of the ideas that were current before 1914.

[2] W. Conze, *loc. cit.*, p. 368.

speak of pure cynicism[1] would certainly be an unjustified over-simplification.

Our aim was to mark out a third domain of freedom and diversity between the uniformity of Russian bureaucracy and Anglo-Saxon social forms. Naturally, in thinking of this third domain we instinctively thought of territories outside Europe. But perhaps European territories could be included as well?

To answer this question we must now examine our European policies. Our world politics could be described as the gleaming obverse of the bright, newly-struck medal of German imperialism. By comparison our European policies would then be the dull reverse. Until this time they had been determined by an unequivocal, typically continental policy of expediency, but we now needed to formulate new policies with wider aims embracing, even subordinating, continental policies. They remained the same, of course, in so far as they still regarded Germany as having reached her territorial saturation point on the continent. Yet they were different; for to pursue its world policies, the Reich had to be strong enough to secure its base in Europe. It must not, as it were, lose its balance as it reached out of the window of Europe for the fruit far away. At this point, however, new considerations

---

[1] According to P. Rohrbach, Friedrich Naumann once formulated Germany's task in the following terms: "We Germans must have something to regard as our own special task in the history of the world—some task that nobody else can fulfil as well as we. We need a national vocation within the household of universal humanity, so that we may be able to stand up for our national independence with all our heart and soul. Our faith in nationalism and our faith in humanity are for us two sides of the same question."

89

forced their way into our European policies. The rivalry with England that we had kindled in the world at large blew back on to the continent.

Here Bismarck had already won the Reich a privileged position which, by this time, was leading to talk —exaggerated though it might be—of German hegemony. But surely the Reich had only adopted this position by agreement with England, and as a bastion to help defend the island against anti-English tendencies in France and Russia. Now it was a question of maintaining this position even without English goodwill or, in other words, of eliminating the balance of power which, so the skilful English politicians had claimed, they were entitled to manipulate for their own safety. This aim could be achieved in one of two ways. Either a European front could be formed under German leadership to exclude England from the continent, or alternatively an alliance to draw Germany closer to England; but such an alliance must assure the Reich the upper hand and not debase it to the status of a continental sword in defence of England by limiting its naval armament—as Chamberlain's offers seemed to imply.[1] In either case our main interest was to ensure that our world politics should not suffer any setback in Europe.

What in fact took place was the exact opposite. Through the "encirclement" England succeeded in turning the balance of power against Germany, thus upsetting the calculations which the Germans had made at the beginning of the cold war. But it was

[1] As late as 1916 Otto Hintze expressed satisfaction that at the turn of the century, the Reich had not yielded to the temptations of English diplomacy and had not renounced naval armament. Cf. also Hallgarten, *Imperialismus* (1951), pp. 382, 422.

already apparent that our imperialists stood firm in their determination to follow exactly the course that they had previously chosen, even at the risk of a great war in Europe—a risk which German public opinion had watched, defiantly and fatalistically, approaching since Agadir. In the last resort the public was prepared to pay even this price, as long as it did not have to abandon our candidacy for world power and a place in world politics. In other words, at this late stage popular imagination was still held prisoner by its preoccupation with the great world outside. The struggle that might be approaching in Europe would amount to no more than a means to clear our path into the world beyond. So it was that, on the brink of the war in Europe, we still had only a negative aim—to try to ensure that the achievement of our positive aim in the world at large should not be frustrated in Europe.

The publicists on the other side who, after the war, charged us with the intention of touching off the hot war, totally misunderstood our whole strategy in the cold war. But the German defence against this charge did not contribute to an uninhibited understanding of our policies either. It made them seem harmless by displaying only their peaceful side, while drawing a veil over their ultimate offensive aims, and, in doing so, made it more difficult to understand the sense and context of the measures we took. Everything haphazard, accidental or personal in these measures was made to appear crucial. The Emperor and the Pan-German League were sent into the wilderness, and the concept of the nation as a responsible, collective personality was as far as possible eliminated. So a water-tight case emerged. Point by point it was true, and yet it did not add up to that truth which satisfies the mind of the historian.

(c)

If we now cross the threshold of 1914, we see immediately what confusion the outbreak of the war was bound to cause in our spiritual armoury; for as soon as our maritime policies were transferred on to the battlefields of the continent, they were also robbed of their spiritual basis. We had been able to present ourselves with some justification as the advocates of the underprivileged nations throughout the world; but could a similar claim hope to find a credulous audience in Europe? Delbrück and his friends had had to point out again and again how gravely Germany's actions against Poland, Denmark and Alsace-Lorraine had damaged the liberal prestige of the Reich among its neighbours. Then, in 1914, came the invasion of Belgium. How could we possibly justify our European policies with the same liberal ideas that we had prepared for our world policies? What in fact were our positive aims in Europe? When our government was called upon to speak of them, it was patently embarrassed. Of course public opinion was largely in agreement on the ultimate imperialist aim, the demand for "freedom of the seas" which implicitly included the destruction of English maritime supremacy;[1] but on the new and immediate aims to be

[1] As late as August 1915 even the Socialists, including the Haase group, agreed on a resolution that demanded, amongst other things, freedom of the seas, the nullification of the right of prize at sea, and the internationalization of the most important sea passages. Though the world system of states that they hoped

achieved, a variety of improvised opinions spread out like a fan. Naturally everyone wanted to guarantee that no threat could re-emerge on the continent, but judgements as to the nature and the measure of such a guarantee differed according to party tendencies and the changing fortunes of the military campaigns. Compared with the absolutely immutable ultimate goal, this guarantee undoubtedly never amounted to more than a relative, temporary aim. In striking contrast to our enemies' stirring demands for Strassburg, Trieste or Constantinople, our own immediate European aims had no higher justification than mere expediency in promoting our ultimate aim of world power for Germany.

It was especially in the West that the idealistic, liberal formulas of our imperialists failed us completely. In attacking England, we were attacking the smaller European nations' most obvious historic defender— that is, the island kingdom and the balance of power that it maintained. The forcible elimination of this balance and of its island guarantor would automatically lead to German supremacy, with all its inherent threats to the sovereignty of every one of the smaller states.[1]

to see established bore certain federalist traits, which distinguished it from the projects of the bourgeois imperialists, both sides nevertheless agreed on the most important point—their common desire to eliminate English maritime supremacy.

[1] Characteristically, one place where this emerges is in the demands that Bethmann-Hollweg made in December 1915 in a conversation with Scheidemann. He demanded that the wall that Germany used to protect herself must be as strong as the hatred of her enemies. Military, political and economic assurances must be used to make the small nations harmless as English outposts. (Cf. *Das Werk des Untersuchungs-ausschusses*, XII, I, p. 63.)

Tirpitz, amongst others, never understood that the ideas of

The fact that German policies tended in the same direction in the years before the war had not necessarily been a cause for alarm precisely because the balance of power had been effective. A German victory, however, would make her neighbours' prospects extremely gloomy, even if she renounced all territorial annexations. But would she renounce them? And if so, for how long? Huge demands for annexations, proceeding from the Pan-German storm-centre, suddenly raised large sections of German public opinion to fever pitch. We were half forced and half frightened into trying somehow to justify a supra-national power in Europe; but thereupon the arguments that we had grown accustomed to using against any supra-national power wielded by our enemies, the imperial powers in the world outside, could no longer be applied with a clear conscience.

On the contrary, these arguments now turned against us, and the liberal imperialists especially were to experience their boomerang effect. As soon as the defence of our own national existence involved injury

freedom formulated before 1914 for use in the world outside Europe could never hope to make any impression in Europe after 1914, and especially not in Western Europe. Our propaganda, he said, should have impressed our mission on the other nations of the European continent. It should have encouraged them to stand up for the freedom of Europe against the giant powers beyond the seas—the Anglo-Saxons (not, of course, the Russians) —who were holding the nations in physical and spiritual subjection. Of course Tirpitz was not alone in his lack of understanding of what could be achieved by even the most skilful German propaganda. There are hints of similar ideas even in the writings of Max Weber. Above all they appear in the work of Max Scheler, e.g. in *Krieg und Aufbau* (1916); with the additional idea, which can be made to justify the concession of different degrees of freedom, that different nations are of different value.

to other nations, these liberal imperialists were faced with a moral dilemma, a conflict with their highest convictions. There was a latent weakness in the inability of German ideology to base itself on an idea with some fundamental appeal. Spanish ideology had once been able to do this through the Counter-Reformation; the French, later, through the Revolution; the Anglo-Saxons at this moment, thanks to the freedom implicit in an island existence; and the Russians were soon to do it through Communism. Germany, however, had no comparable tangible mission to offer to humanity as a whole.

She could offer no better justification for her drive to power than the memory of the role which Fichte and Hegel had promised the Germans a hundred years before. She was to be the current bearer of the torch of humanity. But a hundred years earlier the concept of Germany as the torch-bearer was based on pride in the flowering of the German mind. Could the German mind at the beginning of the twentieth century still compete as dazzlingly as it had at the beginning of the nineteenth? Had it committed itself absolutely to imperialistic ambitions? Ranke said: "A great people, like an independent state, is recognized not only by its ability to hold its enemies behind their frontiers. The essential foundation of its existence is that it should furnish a new expression of the human spirit. . . . This is its God-given task." We did not realize that there was such a task inherent in our improvised policies aimed at European hegemony. Instead, we felt that we had been forced on to the spiritual defensive and thought ourselves obliged to explain why Western civil liberties had been limited in our country by authority. In short, German individualism became the subject of intellectual doubts.[1] How could we possibly hope, then, to develop sufficient powers of attraction to carry the free nations of Western Europe along with us? What was the outcome of all this? Again and again we simply appealed to the right of might which, at best, we camouflaged as the ability to guarantee to the disrupted Old World Roman order[2] and a *pax Romana*.[3] We positively boasted of our pure power politics which, we said, were "based on a *raison d'état*", calmly and proudly refusing to provide ideological justifications such as the West advanced and we branded as mere Machiavellian dissimulation of egotistical interests. We were proud of the ruthless objectivity of our "Prussian stamp".

Nor did this objectivity gain in human warmth or attractiveness when, in our desire to see Germany in the idealized role of a model internationally-minded nation in the early nineteenth-century sense of the term, we tried to link objectivity with Socialism. Of course Prussianism and Socialism were beginning to merge (and to foreshadow the tendencies of the Third Reich). But what became of the liberal, the humanitarian and the revolutionary elements of Socialism in the course of this fusion? Max Scheler interpreted the rise of Germany as the rise of the fourth estate, whose revolutionary ethos of work was expelling the Western

[1] Significant evidence of this defensive attitude can be seen in the five lectures on German Freedom, published in 1917, and especially in Meinecke's and Troeltsch's contributions.

[2] These words were used by Rudolf Borchardt in 1914 in a war speech.

[3] R. Koser, at the time of his last illness (according to his family).

beati possidentes of the third estate from their paradise. In much the same way Paul Lensch, himself a Socialist, simply equated the World Revolution with the victory of a powerful Germany. Thus revolutionary Marxism found no room to develop in the authoritarian land of its conception. It did not become Germany's mission, as Marx had hoped it would. The only element of Marxism that was to mature in Germany was the heritage of the Hegelian idea of power contained within it, and this took the form of visions of the total organization of state and economy. These visions were formulated in Plenge's *Ideen von 1914*, an impromptu study of the beginning of the war which was a product of the same painful feeling that a mission on the continent of Europe was totally lacking. Nevertheless, there was no hiding the fact that we really had no spiritual weapon comparable with those of the Western Powers.

Two exceptions, Ireland and Flanders, only prove the rule. In Ireland the respective roles of Germany and England were reversed; England was the dangerous, hated neighbour on land, Germany the protector beyond the sea. In Flanders we tried to fill the role of the kind uncle—not unsuccessfully, as long as things went well for us. But these two exceptions could not begin to dispel the bleakness on our ideological front in the West.

The position on the Eastern front, on the other hand, was altogether more favourable. The kind of opportunity that was exceptional in the West, was the general rule in the East. On the under-developed fringe of Europe our ideology preserved some of the attraction that it certainly possessed outside Europe.

The Czarist Empire made an ideally sinister foil: the decline of the level of civilization towards the East and the traditions of the West both favoured our ideology. We felt that the peripheral nations might provide a suitable battle-ground for a trial of strength between the explosive liberal power inherent in the principle of nationalism and the Eastern *imperium.*

This, at any rate, was the great hope cherished by our liberal imperialists. They were happy to be able to carry on the struggle that had been forced upon them with a clear conscience, at least in this area. For here, in their opinion, their motives in the sphere of power politics coincided exactly with their ideals: Germany's egotistical, nationalist interest in security coincided with the altruistic nationalist principle of the universal freedom of nations. Delbrück, for example, was convinced that the claims of the peripheral nations to self-determination were in accord with German interests. "Germany's great idealistic aim must be to guarantee the freedom and independence of the smaller nations, not only her own. Every nation shall be as free as we are."[1]

Since in the East their dreams had some foundation in fact, the liberal imperialists were delighted to shift their emphasis from West to East. We have seen how, before the war, they had looked expectantly to the West and to the oceans. Once the war had begun, however, it not only proved more and more difficult to force a decision in the West but, to a liberal eye, the conflict itself assumed an increasingly unpleasant aspect. If violence were done to free nations in the

[1] H. Delbrück before the Committee of Investigation; *loc. cit.*, pp. 51 ff.

West, the sacred principle of the nation state would be defiled, our ideological foundations cut away and the seeds of future disaster sown. One day these violated national feelings would rise against Germany as they had against Napoleon; Delbrück's greatest fear had always been the possibility that the German Reich might be forced or lured into the path of the First French Empire. From this point of view he felt that even a victory over England had its dangers, although he must secretly have admitted that the world power that he wanted for Germany could never flourish without the safeguard of a certain degree of supremacy in Europe, such as Bismarck's Reich had enjoyed. But this supremacy was to be as unobtrusive as possible, and was not to provoke the resistance of the whole Western world, including America; it was not, in fact, to achieve by force what would be bound to occur gradually and peacefully in the normal course of development. Hence his efforts to stop the hot war in the West by a negotiated peace before it set off destructive chain-reactions. He and his friends were perfectly willing to accept a return to the *status quo* through a Hubertusburg peace, made more palatable, if possible, by colonial gains in Africa—especially as such a return would permit a return to the cold war, in which final victory would be certain once the hot attack had been repulsed. We should insure ourselves against a second attack by improving our position in the east, where, in contrast to the West, the liberal nationalism of neighbouring nations spoke for us, not against us, and where a genuine universal mission could help us to further our own interests.

In actual fact our interests and our mission were in

contradiction with one another even in the east. The harmony between the two that the liberals had so confidently foreseen failed to prevail as unequivocally as they had imagined. They were inclined to lay the blame for this on the short-sightedness of official governing circles among the Central Powers. But was this the root of the problem? Surely it lay deeper. The special treatment that the two Central Powers reserved for their Polish possessions could not easily be dismissed as short-sightedness, yet it rendered unconvincing their role of liberators of Russian Poland—a role which they assumed only belatedly and unwillingly, and which contradicted their traditional policy of co-operation with the third partitioning power and, even more, Prussian ambitions of Germanization. Moreover, Austria's special concern for the large Polish landowners in eastern Galicia made the German block less attractive to the Ukrainians, and Germany's consideration for the Teutonic barons had the same effect on the three small Baltic nations. But the greatest difficulties were naturally encountered in the Balkans: if the Habsburg Empire were to survive, there could be no possibility of free development in the Empire for the southern Slavs and the Roumanians, not to mention the Slav populations which had been completely incorporated.

One general source of friction lay concealed beneath all these various specific problems. The western concept of nationality, as it survived in liberal ideology, could not be applied to the east without disrupting the general pattern of life there, because the stratifications and the confused interplay of nations at different stages of consciousness could never conform to the concept of nationality as understood by the west. If none the less the attempt were made, it would rouse chaotic desires which Germany would never be able to satisfy, however unselfish she might become.

In the north the situation was more promising. In Finland we were able to play the role of liberator consistently. Neither contradictions between our role and our interests, nor mixed populations, could embarrass us. Here too there was some mixture of population, but this could not confuse the issue sufficiently to outweigh the favourable discussion our mission evoked in Sweden. Here, and virtually only here, our mission won a convinced and considerable following. Our claim to be delimiting a third area, an area of freedom and diversity between the Russian and the Anglo-Saxon spheres, could easily be made to harmonize with Sweden's own desire to assert herself between East and West, for at that time Germany's power, held at a safe distance south of Sweden by the sea, presented no acute danger. Neither Sweden nor Finland was really our neighbour, and their relationship to our supremacy on the continent was therefore comparable with that of Ireland. They were more amenable to our ideas than the continental nations in the narrower sense of the term— even than those in the east.

Quite apart from this exception in the north, the liberals had another very powerful argument in the east; one to which we have devoted too little attention so far, and with which they hoped to reconcile the contradictions in their ideology. We have already mentioned the sinister foil represented by the Czarist Empire. But—the argument now ran—this foil involved not only a foreign domination that could be removed once for all, but also the eternal danger of its recurrence. Without a strong Germany to protect them, the peripheral nations would be doomed to defeat. If they wished to preserve their independence against Russia, they must be prepared to allow Germany to limit that independence to some extent. In other words, Germany was justifying her own claims to security and expansion in the east by citing her function as the bastion of the West against the eastern barbarians.

This function was in some ways a re-statement of the ideological task that the Democrats had proclaimed for Germany in 1848—though at that time the situation did not tempt Germany to strive for hegemony or for an independent role between East and West, but rather drew her into the western orbit. Nevertheless, the declaration of war against Russia in 1914 had woken echoes of the scattered traditions of the old brand of German democracy, even if only to enlist the sympathies of the Social Democrats. These traditions also lent a greater degree of sanctity to our organization of what one might call a defensive belt of more or less independent states on the eastern and south-eastern outworks of the Central Powers. They even survived in the *grand dessin* of Central Europe that the liberals now envisaged as a possible elastic and organic solution of all Germany's problems—in the spheres of power and of ideas, in European politics and in world politics. In terms of world politics, this solution offered us a well-defined sphere which would constitute a great supra-national, imperial area and could also serve as a secure base for further imperialistic expansion outside Europe. In European politics, it assured us a sufficient

degree of unobtrusive supremacy to allow us to eliminate the old balance of power controlled by England
without setting off any disastrous reactions among our
neighbours. In fact, it was argued, even our neighbours must ultimately realize that a German bulwark
stretching from the Baltic to the Mediterranean would
protect them against a Russian flood—a flood which,
in view of the inevitable rise of the civilizations of the
vast expanses of Eurasia, could only be prevented by
defence on a grand scale.[1]

Seen in this light, the Russian danger could provide
German power with a real *raison d'être*. It seemed to
provide the idea of German supremacy in Europe with
the message that it lacked, and to fill the vacuum which
resulted in 1914 from the collapse of the idea of an
imperialistic mission. What a *volte-face* this was.
German imperialism, which had set out in 1900 looking westwards to destroy English maritime supremacy,

[1] Max Scheler gave impressive utterance to similar ideas in
Genius des Krieges (1917). His fundamental idea was that the
European balance of power should be eliminated and that the
whole continent should combine against Russia under German
leadership. During the war the demand that the European balance
of power should be eliminated was expressed repeatedly on all
sides; indeed, to some extent it was only at this time that it was
recognized as a logical German demand. Delbrück expressed himself very carefully and made it look as though he believed that a
European and a world balance of power could exist side by side.
P. Lensch, Hintze and Oncken, on the other hand, saw matters
quite clearly. Friedrich von Bernhardi, the Pan-German, made no
secret of the fact even before the war that Germany would have
to destroy the European balance if she wanted to become a world
power. Nor did Paul Rohrbach, as can be seen in *Deutschland
unter den Weltvölkern*. The fact that even the political leaders had
been pursuing similar ideas for some time can be seen in E. von
Veitsch, *Das europäische Gleichgewicht* (1941). The author gives
some early evidence on pp. 297 and 301.

now faced east towards the continent. Once again we see the development which was typical of all previous wars for hegemony and which was even to characterize the second World War; we see the result of the usual failure in the struggle against our main island enemy in the west.

But this development shows that such a *volte-face* offered no way out of the labyrinth of the war for hegemony. England would not renounce the overthrow of the Central Powers on the continent for fear that she might not be able to oppose them there with a sufficiently strong coalition in a future war, while Germany would not renounce the possibility of achieving her ambitions at a later, more favourable opportunity, either peacefully[1] or by force of arms. Even the liberals were not willing to make this renunciation. We must repeat yet again that it never occurred to them that they might permanently give up their claim to form a third force between East and West. They did not dream, as they had in 1848, of opting for the West; for how could they do so without suffering crippling losses? Once adopted, the policy of *carte blanche* could not easily be rejected. "We are free to take the former course, but the latter makes us slaves."

However ardently the liberals might propagate Germany's anti-Russian mission, clearly they could not hope in this way to make any impression on the determination of the West, for the mission bore all too

[1] Tirpitz, in *Erinnerungen*, p. 261, says that in 1916 the Foreign Ministry was trying to achieve victory over the Russians because victory over the English was impossible, but that it intended to continue its policy of gradually overshadowing England after the war.

obviously the stamp of pure improvisation. Prussia and Germany had risen as a continental power with Russian support, and although the foundation of the Reich had contributed to Russo-German tension—a logical development neither expected nor desired—in the last analysis only German aspirations in world politics had increased this tension to the point of war.[1] Our anti-Russian mission, then, was anything but long-standing. Before 1914 we had obviously not taken the Russian peril seriously, and even after the beginning of the war we would have preferred to exorcise it by co-operation, either on the basis of the conservative, Prussian, continental tradition or on the basis of our new maritime ambitions (Tirpitz). Compared with ours, England's anti-Russian attitude was much older. It had been the natural corollary of England's maritime empire since the late eighteenth century and had only occasionally been interrupted when the two powers on the outer wings of Europe formed alliances against the common danger of a traditional hegemony over the continent, exercised a hundred years before by France and now by Germany. When, in spite of this, the France of Napoleon, the Germany of Wilhelm, and later Hitler's too, maintained that they were leading and protecting the West against the threat from the East, they were acting like a man who sets the house on fire and then invites the other occupants to help him put it out.

[1] In 1915 R. von Kühlmann said to Meinecke that Russia had only dared to declare war because she was certain that England would join her. (A direct consequence of our aspirations in the sphere of world politics.)

(d)

If we look again at all these twentieth-century ideas which aimed to extend the nineteenth-century concept of the nation state, we become keenly conscious of the gross disproportion between our physical and our spiritual energies. Our pre-war imperialism succeeded in creating some kind of spiritual harmony between its own aims in the world and the ambitions of the nations outside Europe, and in extracting a world mission out of our particular mode of thought. But such a mission could never hope to be sufficiently attractive to compete with those of other nations, especially the English. Moreover, this schematic mission looked even less convincing when the war, which we did not want and which therefore caught us spiritually unprepared, became centred in Europe. Once our liberals were forced to try to win some kind of supremacy on the continent, they became involved in painful conflict with their innermost convictions instead of sweeping other nations along with these convictions. Harder pressed by their enemies' ideas than by their arms, especially in the West, they found in the East the only sector where they could improvise some kind of mission, and even this was insufficient to give this war for hegemony any comprehensive spiritual basis.

How different had been the position for previous supreme powers. They had been able to call on the Counter-Reformation, French universal civilization, or the achievements of the Revolution as ideals to precede their armies, spread their messages, survive even the excessive demands made on them in unsuccessful conflicts, outlive defeat, and so maintain a faithful body of partisans even beyond their own frontiers. (How different also is the position of the two giants of today, each facing the other on the firm basis of different missions.) In the words of Dostoevsky, we were able to protest in our own name, but not to inspire in others the faith which would carry them along with us, the faith that "we had the final answer for the world, and, at the head of the assembled nations, could lead it to its predestined goal". We could not offer any "God-given task" in Ranke's sense nor, in Hegel's, could we embody "a moment that, because it represents the present stage of the idea of the world spirit, can claim to exercise absolute rights over all others". We could not give concrete form to our traditional concept of Germany as the bearer of the torch of humanity destined to restore the world to health (Emanuel Geibel). "What use is an obstinate conviction that one day one will again be in a position to speak and to lead mankind, if one cannot speak at the decisive moment?" (Thomas Mann). The coffin of Germany's might had only a modest cortège in 1918—and in 1944 it was even more modest.

I need hardly explain that the weakness of our mission cannot have been due to any inherent weakness in our national spiritual energies. On the contrary, Germany was spiritually richer than any other country in the world at the beginning of the nineteenth century, and she was still second to none at the beginning of the twentieth. No: the cause was the peculiarly German tendency to isolate spiritual matters from questions of political power—that lack of inner harmony which had characterized our history from the time of the Hohenstauffens and which could never be repaired once the foundation of the Prussian Reich had been super-imposed upon it. The river-bed of Prussianism, so artificially restricted, had never offered sufficient scope to the German spirit, and under the pressure tragically applied at the time of the first World War, all the cracks in our sub-strata burst open.

We have described the efforts of our nation to justify, ennoble or moderate, by means of supra-national and idealistic concepts, its elemental urge to achieve power; but it would be wrong for us simply to note their failure. Inherent in these efforts are powers which, if released from the hybrid, egocentric conditions of their time, may help us in our fight to create a new and broader western society with deeper roots. For the comforting aspect of our discordant history is that it offers a far better opportunity for a new start than does the harmonious history of happier nations.

VERSAILLES
AFTER THIRTY-FIVE YEARS

THE traveller to Italy who approaches the St. Gotthard pass by rail will be struck by the church at Wassen. He will see it first from close to, in the narrow Reuss valley, and then a second time, set in the widening mountain panorama, as he comes out of a spiral tunnel. Older people are in the same position today with regard to the Treaty of Versailles. It first loomed up suddenly, terrifyingly close, just over a generation ago; now, after coming through the dark spiral of the Third Reich, we look down upon it a second time from the heights of our terrible experience, and see it set in an historical mountain panorama which we could not survey from the narrow valley of our youth.

At that time we had only the memory of the great European peace treaties of the past to help us to comprehend the incomprehensible. First there was the Treaty of Münster which, though it emerged from an entirely different context, seemed to us in our bitter despair to be related to Versailles. Then there was the Vienna Settlement, which was certainly a parallel to Versailles; but by comparison Vienna was the bright side of the moon—not only in the eyes of the losers, but soon in the victors' too.

For a hundred years the world had thought differently of the Vienna Settlement. This was natural and understandable in the case of the French, the

defeated supreme power; but the nationalist expectations of the Germans were disappointed too in 1815—
not to mention those of the Italians and the Poles.
Ultimately the liberals and democrats of the whole
world agreed in condemning the peace-makers of the
dancing congress and their concept of Restoration. Only
after the first World War were the Metternichs and
the Castlereaghs to enjoy their reinstatement; for they
had succeeded in bringing about a lasting peace such
as nobody with any insight could expect from the
Treaties of the Parisian Suburbs.

Today we naturally tend to feel that this belated
justice towards Vienna involved an injustice towards
Versailles, for while the analogies between the two
were recognized, the differences were underrated. The
most important of these differences was that treaties
could more easily be made to last in the age of the
stage-coach, and even of the steam-engine, than in the
age of the internal combustion engine. Compared with
the instability of the twentieth century, the agrarian
and early industrial part of the nineteenth century had
considerable stability. In the nineteenth century there
were still a number of powerful states helping to maintain the balance. Europe's supremacy in the world
was perfectly secure, and there were still very few
Cassandras sounding warnings about the future role of
the world beyond. The United States still lay far off on
the horizon, whereas Russia was close at hand, a considerable European power in the process of becoming
even more European.

In this context the main problem of the Peace Treaty
was from the very first much easier to solve. The
problem was to make it impossible for the defeated

supreme power to plunge Europe into a new war for hegemony.

At least on land, France had been defeated essentially by European continental powers which, long after the conclusion of peace, still had their rifles at the ready to prevent a recurrence of the disaster. The concept of Restoration acted as a cement to hold together all the nations of Europe, including even Restoration France. From the very first France was assured of an honoured place in the Pentarchy, for she represented an essential factor in the general balance of power. So that she might come to terms with her fate, the defeated power was allowed a peaceful, honourable and wealthy existence. After 25 years of war and a struggle of 150 years for European hegemony, the French nation had finally passed the peak of her vitality, so that she was never again able to summon sufficient determination to renew the struggle for supremacy, though she tried repeatedly to do so—in 1830, 1840, 1848 and at various times under Napoleon III.

Thus the Vienna Settlement succeeded in fulfilling the two contrasting requirements that must be fulfilled if a peace treaty is to have any hope of lasting. It was sufficiently reconciliatory towards the defeated power on the one hand, yet sufficiently stern on the other, to ensure by one or other of these two means that the treaty could not be violated.

The Treaty of Versailles was very different: not because the peace-makers were so much less wise than their predecessors at Vienna, but because they had to overcome difficulties that were not only different in degree, but also in kind. Justice demands that this be recognized, even if the comparison, in itself so fruitful, should make our verdict less, not more, favourable. Let us follow it through objectively, point by point.

The first factor we encounter is the dynamism of modern civilization, trying with explosive force to wreck the delicate network of Europe's old political frontiers and producing a thousand different manifestations of the economic, social and political instability on which Marxism had always counted. Secondly, there was the annihilation of Austria-Hungary, the great power which, a hundred years earlier, had acted as mediator between the opposing factions. Thirdly, there was the withdrawal of Russia from the zone of the peripheral nations. Where those two powers had stood, there were now young improvised creations with no stability of their own and therefore hardly able to maintain a stable equilibrium. Germany had taken it upon herself to eliminate the balance of power and to replace it with a world balance of power in which she should have a place. With her titanic force she had been as successful in achieving the negative aspect of this programme as she had been unsuccessful in achieving the positive end. The old continent lay dead in its own blood, and even the British Isles had suffered terribly. However, the profit from the passing of Europe did not fall to a powerful, diverse world system of states such as we had believed would succeed the European system. On the contrary, the new outlines of the dualism produced by a world torn between the hostile spheres of freedom and Communism, with the simmering revolution of the coloured world between the two, were already beginning to set their mark on all political forms everywhere. Thus a prospect opened which could not have been foreseen at Vienna, and it raised not only old difficulties in new and more complicated forms, but difficulties of a completely new kind. It became apparent that this time the problem was not to provide a new European order after a European war, but to create a new World Order after a World War. A sober comparison between the Congress of Vienna and the congress in Paris shows that the tasks confronting the two were indeed related to a significant degree, but that, to a much greater degree, the statesmen of Versailles faced unfamiliar problems half shrouded in swirling mists—problems that could not be taken in at a single glance.

In this unstable context the old, but still the main, problem in drawing up any peace treaty—to prevent the defeated power from resuming its fight for hegemony—was far more difficult to solve than it had been at Vienna. For this time the supreme power had not been defeated mainly by the continental powers, but only after the unprecedented intervention of the Americans. There were therefore no continental powers to guarantee the peace as there had been in 1815. Defeated Russia was just as interested in nullifying the peace treaty as was her defeated enemy Germany, and the combined interest of these two amounted to a danger of the first order—and not only for Europe. What about France? She, of course, owed her victory to Anglo-Saxon aid rather than to her own strength. As for the improvised creations of central and eastern Europe, they needed support more than they could give it.

Finally, there was another special and extremely important factor. Whereas in 1815 France had passed the peak of her vitality, it was only during the World

War that Germany had become fully aware of her energies. She was only at the beginning of her struggle for hegemony: France in 1815 was at the end of hers.

What was the logical result of all this? This time it was impossible to prevent the resurgence of the defeated power simply by setting up a continental balance. More was required: namely that the Anglo-Saxons on both sides of the ocean, whose unpremeditated efforts had determined the outcome of the first World War, should also be prepared to work more systematically to determine the nature of the peace. The framework of Europe had become too small to guarantee the pacification of the defeated Titans. Only the Western world as a whole could guarantee this. The subject for debate was Euramerica, the *imperium Anglo-Saxonicum* as a great dome sheltering the whole free world including Europe. The flood had spread so far since 1917, when it might still have been dammed, that the resulting unprecedented situation could only be brought under control by some correspondingly unprecedented concept. This concept had to be wide enough to solve both the old problem of pacifying Europe and the new one of drawing the venom out of global dualism and the coloured movement. The old problem, the pacification of Europe, which the island nation had so often sought to solve by preventing the rise of any new supremacy from within the continent, was now to be solved by a new kind of loose hegemony exercised over the continent from outside by the Anglo-Saxons themselves: the old end was to be achieved by new means. The play of forces on the continent was to be brought to a standstill and, instead, preparations were to be made for the peaceful amalgamation of the

114

forces of the whole free Atlantic West. In this way the new tasks in the world at large would also be tackled, and both the Communist and the coloured problems faced.

The problem was to create not only a political synthesis, but also a spiritual one. In 1815 the idea of Restoration had provided a cement to hold the new structure together. The need for a spiritual cement of this kind was even greater in 1918, for this time the Revolution had not been quashed. One of the fateful differences between 1815 and 1918 was that in 1918 a Revolution beyond Western control had just flared up: the Communist Revolution.

There could be no doubt that this spiritual synthesis, as well as the political one, must come mainly from the English. Their great moment of responsibility to the world had undeniably come; they now embodied the fate of the West, both in the wider and the narrower senses of the term. From their original position on the fringe, they had moved into the centre where decisions are made. They alone had risen uninterruptedly for centuries, facing first the Spaniards, then the French, then the Germans as their enemies —and now they had to face the Russians, emerging even more ominously and moving similarly from the fringe to the centre.

It is easy to be wise after the event and to formulate the aims of the peace-makers of Versailles now that so many years have elapsed. Instead, let us ask how they themselves saw these aims: what they wanted, and what they did. We must look first at the Anglo-Saxons —an ellipse with two foci, of which the American seemed initially to capture the limelight much more than the British. But the British, with an Empire both white and coloured which formed part of the world outside Europe, at the same time bridged the gap between that world and the group of continental victors, especially France and Italy. Behind these victors the states and peoples of central, eastern and south-eastern Europe were ranged more like pawns subject to the decisions of others than full participants.

America, or more precisely Wilson, was indeed the bearer of a concept of unprecedented boldness: originally sketched only lightly to stimulate ideas, yet sufficiently broad and ambitious to embrace both European and world problems and to dominate them from a central eminence. Since it was an Anglo-Saxon project, it had roots in the British sphere too and reflected that idealistic aspect of the Anglo-Saxon mentality which Continentals so often deprecate as cant or excessive crusading zeal. With a single disdainful stroke it closed the books on the whole history of the continent with its continual struggles for power. It was a negation of the free balance of power, out of which the wars for hegemony had grown and to which they always reverted, and it was a negation of the old military monarchies. It did not aim at a new, but still unstable, balance of power between victors and vanquished, but rather, in one bold sweep, at stability and justice for the whole world. It aimed to give logical reality to the principle of nationality. Its aims were not merely an armistice, but a lasting peace; the peaceful resolution of possible differences through the supranational democratic forms of the League of Nations; the protection of minorities by the extension of national self-determination; universal disarmament;

finally, the birth of a new phase of history and a new form of international law. What had been realized in America through the Constitution was to be realized the world over through the League of Nations, which was an expression of all the Anglo-Saxon ideals of freedom—both human and political. The League was to refresh the stagnant air of the continent, to oppose Communism with a front of purified faith and the Revolution of the masses with a revolution of rejuvenated Westernism. And under the banner of justice the support of the coloured races might be enlisted, and the injustices of colonialism extirpated.

This was indeed a stimulating project, but how was it to be endued with the colours of reality? Was it enough that the existing forms in Europe had been shattered and that the Americans commanded sufficient revolutionary ideas to create new forms?

The beginnings were extremely promising. The tormented masses of Europe seemed willing to allow themselves to be poured into new moulds, and the United States, with their decisive military successes and the charismatic authority of their President, seemed to possess the necessary qualities to undertake a successful re-casting.

But it is common knowledge how quickly these promising beginnings proved fruitless and the wave of this idealistic concept broke and disappeared in spray against a range of cliffs.

It struck the first cliffs straight away in the shape of the British. There were the demands of the Dominions for German overseas possessions, met with the outward sanctity of the mandates. There were secret treaties which tied the mother country's hands in Europe, and finally there were the expectations of reparations which were cherished by the masses in England and had somehow to be satisfied. On the whole, however, England stood within the same ellipse as the United States. Once her maritime position, over which the war had broken out, was assured, she could again maintain equilibrium on the continent from the distance of her island, though now her purpose was not so much to maintain a balance between Germany and France as to contain Russia. It had been a constant feature of the island kingdom's broad and far-sighted policies to provide for defence against her Eastern rival in the world, once the struggle for hegemony in the older part of Europe had been halted. With this purpose in mind it was important for the British not to drive Germany to despair or into the arms of Bolshevism, and to preserve her bourgeois social forms—though not, of course, her incalculable military potential. Thus Lloyd George spoke against France and Poland in favour of sparing Germany both on the Rhine and on the Vistula, and not just as a realist but also—let us admit it—as an idealist, as the advocate of the island's ethic of justice and of that fair play which is foreign to the nature of the Continental.

The greatest danger was not to be Germany but the continental mentality. It was of course in Germany's recent supremacy that continental belligerence had just been manifest in its most frightening form, but what could be more welcome to the vanquished, after the annihilation of the basis of their power, than to seek safety on the firm ground of justice and exchange the weapons of war for those of democratic dialectics? Now that their maritime dreams had been shattered, they could move, in the name of self-determination, towards the realization of their older, continental dreams. With the *Anschluss* of their brethren in Austria and Bohemia they could raise their population to almost double that of the apparently victorious French, achieve a new and unrivalled geographic and demographic personality in the old continent of Europe, use it to overshadow the Balkanized buffer zone in central and eastern Europe, and transform their defeat into a spring-board for a new greatness. How much of this thinking should be atttributed at each stage in the development of events to disguised Machiavellianism and how much to stirrings of genuine repentance? This question involves an extremely complicated problem of national psychology. The possibility of repentance should certainly not be too lightly dismissed, for our young nation was capable of change; it was more profoundly shattered than any other, endowed with affinities with the Americans, and well suited to co-operate with them. On the other hand it would be wrong to underrate our unrepentant feeling of strength and that capacity endlessly to pursue the paths of political power, which had always been characteristic of nations supreme on the continent.

This capacity was most clearly to be seen in France. Here the continental mentality was in open conflict with the diametrically opposed trans-atlantic concept. Over the centuries the wars for hegemony had shaped this mentality into a chaotic egotism manifest in every member of the family of nations; and only in the great coalitions created to prevent the hegemony of one nation over the others did this egotism occasionally appear to have been overcome. France in decline could no longer summon sufficient ambition to strive for hegemony herself, but this only made her the more sensitive in observing the ambitions of her more energetic neighbour. In her heart she refused to accept German unity—even the unity of Bismarck's Reich, not to mention the *Anschluss*. Ideally she would have liked to pulverize it in the mortar of another Treaty of Westphalia. With the clairvoyant distrust of those whose fates are linked, she foresaw the mutability of German repentance: it takes a Montague to understand a Capulet. However, this premonition only made her selfishly determined still further to tighten the familiar screws of continental power politics and not to stake her existence on the experiments of American therapy. She obviously owed her salvation to the Anglo-Saxons, and, together in permanent alliance, the three powers should guarantee the peace. But for her the most important condition was that the peace itself must offer some realistic assurance of power in the old style, to which she might possibly add a guarantee of peace.

Another nuance of the continental mentality can be seen in the *sacro egoismo* of the Italians. It was more naïve but no less passionate than the bitter feelings of the waning supreme power, France, and it was no less antagonistic to any Anglo-Saxon idea of justice and no less absolutely determined to squeeze every possible advantage out of secret treaties and the opportunities of the moment.

What could Wilson do against the continental powers? Once again the British had allowed their military power to sink to nothing in the hour of victory. The French, on the other hand, only lashed the tiller tighter, and so the military power relationship between rescuer and rescued was reversed. As a result, even the American threat of a separate peace with Germany lost force. Above all, while the President was fighting on the European front, his foundations at home were crumbling. The traditional rigidity of isolationists was strengthened by their contact with the ungrateful, atavistic rigidity of the continental nations. Wilson therefore had quickly to find some way of protecting the structure of his work. In order to save the centre-piece of his plan, the League of Nations, he had to accept compromises that were painful to him. If the League could be given life, the threshold of a new age would have been crossed in spite of everything, and there would then be some hope of smoothing and chiselling the unevenness of the casting later.

The Europeans did in fact concede the League of Nations to the President as a whim, while he, in return, agreed to much that was against his principles, not only because he was being dragged down in the trail of his sinking star, but partly also through bias and ignorance. Even so, the vanquished and the weak owed him a greater debt of gratitude than they cared to admit; but the victors and the strong were proportionately dissatisfied. Surely this disappointment on both sides is a testimonial to Versailles?

Our verdict today would be different, too, if the Treaties had at least been carried out as the peace-makers intended. It was only the fact that they were not that distorted them and showed up all their failings.

What was the cause of this subsequent disaster? Paradoxically it lay in the very country which had first surprised the world with its grandiose concept.

121

America now surprised the world again by giving it up. The isolationists refused their signature, even to the Charter of the League of Nations. The League only came into the light of day as a miscarriage. The continental mentality, which had already deeply scarred the formulation of the peace, more and more determined its actual operation.

This was an utterly disastrous turn of events. Euramerica dissolved into its component parts. The crippled League of Nations was left incapable of fulfilling its intended function. The decisions of the Treaty, which had been adjusted to the League, now stood like the futile fragments of a gigantic unfinished cathedral. For this reason alone the Balkanization of central and eastern Europe became a grotesque tragedy. The protection of minorities failed, and the principle of disarmament helped the losers to prepare their resurgence. The problem of reparations devolved on France, and its treatment embittered the defeated nations without gaining anything for the victors. The Anglo-Saxon guarantee, on which Clemenceau had counted in return for his renunciation of a Rhineland buffer state, was not honoured. The French, with their power politics which had been partly to blame for the victory of the isolationists, were not able to guarantee *sécurité* by their own methods—less and less so, the more nervously, angrily and exaggeratedly they turned the screws.

The final result of the *fausses couches* of the peace settlement, therefore, was that it entirely failed to fulfil its principal purpose, that of pacifying the great Titan. The German danger might perhaps have been exorcised within the wider framework of a League of

Nations embracing the whole world, but certainly not within the narrow one of a shrunken Europe. The return to the obsolete ideas of the system of the balance of power that resulted from this triumph of the continental mentality, forced the apparent victor, arrogant and nervous, into intolerable proximity with the artificially fettered giant, goaded to the limit and growing conscious of his old strength and new possibilities. From within and without, German politics were forced back on to the old paths of power, towards another trial of strength—one that might unintentionally, perhaps inevitably, end in a last and terrible fight for European hegemony.

This is the kind of picture of Versailles which we have today if we look down from the heights of our terrible experience and, at the same time, take in the mountain panorama unfolding before us ever more frighteningly day by day. It is a picture that holds a warning of dreadful solemnity for anyone who thinks as a Westerner. We must not fail a second time to solve the problem that the present world situation presents, in a different form but at an analogous point in the spiral. Should European and American solidarity fail once more, the day may come when it might be said that "freedom has disappeared from off the face of the earth".

THE PASSING OF
THE EUROPEAN SYSTEM

SINCE 1914 the reputation of historiography has for various reasons diminished. This is especially true in the sphere of politics, principally because in our increasingly technical civilization the balance between static existence and dynamic development is shifting daily in favour of development. However, there is one theatre of the world where the historical and political point of view remains of primary importance even today: that is the European theatre, the territory of the shrunken, obsolete European system of states, the historic birth-place of modern world civilization. Here historiography still has a real function in the forum where public opinion is made—a function which extends beyond the narrow circle of professional historians, and one which should not be renounced in a spirit of comfortable modesty.

The art of drawing lies in omission. Let us be bold and make a rough sketch consisting of the few guiding lines that are essential to an understanding of the present—though they start at the very beginning of the modern period.

What of the problem of European unity? What of the movement to turn Europe, the geographical concept, into an organic living being? Nobody would deny that their classical and Christian heritage has given our nations a common stamp, and that a certain spiritual unity therefore exists. But is this spiritual unity accompanied by any comparable political unity? Yes, in a certain sense; yet it is, as it were, a unity preceded by a minus sign. For the free and sovereign states competing within the European system have in fact always agreed on one point only, the prevention of the unification of the West under one of themselves, to which the others would lose their sovereignty. Whether this state was Spain, France or Germany—that is, at different times the most powerful nation on the continent —grand coalitions were always formed to compass its defeat.

What is the most important reason why, for four centuries, these coalitions were always successful? It was that the grand coalitions always got invincible support from the powers on the western and eastern wings of Europe, first and foremost in the maritime powers of the west, and secondly in the great peripheral continental powers in the east. These were powers which made the growing resources of the territories outside Europe available for the fight against a supreme power within Europe—in the first case, the resources of overseas territories and, in the second, those of the Eurasian continent. The secret of the modern history of our nations is that new weights, taken from the fringes of Europe and from the world beyond, could always be thrown into the scales on the side of the coalitions, until the critical attack had been overcome and the tottering balance restored once more to equilibrium.

However, it was only natural that the powers on the wings should take advantage of this to develop more and more power in the world outside or, in other words, that the European continent should undermine its own position of supremacy. For the rise of England, and of America behind her, to world power, and the corresponding rise of Russia on the other side, were the price that our continent had to pay for preserving the freedom of its individual sovereign states and of its whole system of the balance of power.

But might not these growing world powers on the wings endanger that freedom? They certainly could not before 1945, for as long as there was a danger that our continent might be united under one supreme power (thus itself becoming a world power), the common interest of the world powers already on the scene merely demanded that this danger be eliminated by a maintenance of the balance of power, so that they themselves might be free to expand further in the world outside.

It is only natural that this political system should, in the course of the centuries, have developed a quite peculiar political mentality among its members. This mentality was determined on the one hand by the perpetual suspicion of all members of the circle against whichever state happened to be the most powerful and, on the other, by the supreme struggle for power of each individual member—a struggle limited not by any legal code or concept, but only by the actual resistance offered by the neighbours of each state and, in the last resort, by the universal suspicion which we have already mentioned. It was primarily the fear of the hegemony of one of them, and of the titanic struggles which would result, that controlled the whole system and thus shaped the instincts of this whole family of states. Just as the crystals in a geode face inward towards each other, so the members of our family of states turned their energies inward and against each other, never outward in mutual solidarity, for it was the powers outside, nurtured on European discord, who guaranteed the European system. In exploring the defence against hegemony, we have isolated the most important factor in the modern history of the states of Europe.

From the beginning of the eighteenth century, however, when Russia began to grow in power, a second main factor began slowly to emerge in the troughs between the waves representing the wars for hegemony, and from time to time to oust the first. This factor was the rivalry of the powers on the wings among themselves, both outside and within Europe. In general both these powers were primarily concerned to prevent any of the old continental European powers from achieving hegemony, so that they might meanwhile expand in the world outside; but Russia was simultaneously trying to expand in Europe too. By nature alien to the West, although forming part of its political system, she broke piece after piece off the eastern edge of western Europe and grafted them on to herself.

Compressed into a few sentences, these were the basic outlines of European development from the sixteenth century to 1945. Even these bare outlines, however, are enough to identify the moment when this development was bound to come to an end. The inevitable end came when the Russians and the Anglo-Saxons had grown so powerful in the world that the European powers, still to all intents and purposes, and despite the most appalling struggles, confined within their old frontiers, were by comparison exhausted and dwarfed. As the world powers absorbed the spirit of modern expansionist civilization more and more quickly, this moment approached faster and faster. It was reached in 1945. The turning-point came suddenly, although it had long been in preparation. The European side of the scales became too light and shot upwards, while that of the world powers fell. The relative positions of the two were completely reversed. Events in Europe ceased to be the centre of world events: on the contrary, the latter began to determine the former. The first main factor in modern European history lost its force: the struggle for hegemony waged by the old continental powers had quite obviously been fought to a finish. The second main factor, the conflict between the Anglo-Saxons and the Russians, has undeniably become the most important, both in Europe and in the world beyond. In the process, part of the house of Europe has been reduced to a heap of rubble; the rest stands in ruins, more or less shattered. Neither part has any need at all of the common roof provided by the old system of the balance of power.

The territory east of the Iron Curtain may justly be called a heap of rubble, in which the Russian pick-axes are busy collecting building materials for the gigantic edifice of the U.S.S.R. Continuing their old procedures, the Russians are here alienating another slice of Europe—the largest yet—from the West. The plan itself is not new; only the vehemence with which they are carrying it out is new.

West of the Iron Curtain, where the Anglo-Saxon way of life predominates, the position is different. Until now, the Anglo-Saxons have, for four centuries, renounced all claim to direct mastery on the continent. They have always been the guarantors of our community of free nations, and they have always been closely connected with the free and varied cultural life that comes so readily from competition between different political forms, as it did once before in similar circumstances in ancient Greece. It would therefore have been in character with this Anglo-Saxon way of life to have withdrawn from the continent on a basis of sea and air supremacy, once Germany had been defeated. However, the crucial turning-point of which we have spoken now made this impossible, for the exhausted continent, which this time had contributed much less than in previous crises to the defeat of the power exercising hegemony, could no longer raise itself by its own strength and, left to itself, fell into the danger of becoming a power vacuum to be filled from the east. The conflict between East and West, the remaining factor in world politics, does not permit any space void of power.

Thus the extent of the change can be observed in the fact that the Anglo-Saxons, the traditional opponents of any constellation with supreme power on the continent, have now, under American leadership, themselves been forced from outside into a kind of limited hegemony, playing the role of protective powers maintaining order on the continent. Although their main aim remains the same, they are now working to achieve it within the framework of Eurasia, not, as previously, of Europe. They are still trying to use a system of balance of power to hold the greatest continental power in some kind of check, but now the system that they are hoping to operate is to be a Eurasian one with a reorganized Europe forming only a part. But in order that the dwarfed states of Europe may have at least the limited powers of resistance of a fragment of a greater whole, they must be fused into an organic unity and must face Communism together, for in their previous isolation they have either shown themselves to be powerless or have frittered away their energies in mutual jealousies. But America, the leader of the Anglo-Saxon powers, regards herself merely as the midwife at the birth of this new unification. As soon as it develops its own life and existence, she will again be content to withdraw, though of course with the intention of maintaining the desired balance from the distance of her island continent purely by means of sea and air power, just as England had been able to do for centuries with the European balance of power.

The great question is this. Will the instinctive drive of the continental nations towards sovereign power and freedom, which has so long been fortunate enough to coincide with Anglo-Saxon interests, suddenly subordinate itself to an opposite trend and accept reductions in the freedom of individual nations in order to save the basis of our Western existence—the freedom of man? This certainly places on the peoples of the continent a very sudden demand for an enormous degree of elasticity; but surely it does not do so entirely without preparation?

For over 150 years there has been no lack of occasional trends opposed to the system of the balance of power; and the longing to release ourselves from this system by means of comprehensive peace settlements has burned specially brightly at the end of our suicidal wars for hegemony. This was so after the Napoleonic Wars and again after the first World War; but the longing always faded again as soon as the memory of

the horrors faded. In 1945 the tormented peoples'
yearning welled up once more. Moreover, politics on
the new grand scale offered additional opportunities—
not indeed from the East, where the Western mentality was ruthlessly crushed by Russian reorganization,
but from the West, where the outbreak of the cold
war has forced the Anglo-Saxons to undertake the
reorganization of the remainder of Europe.

Five years have passed since they began this
attempt.[1] The result cannot yet be seen, so that it is
still too early to give an historical verdict. However,
this only makes the need for a combined political and
historical survey more urgent.

The last five years can fairly easily be divided into
two phases of approximately equal length. In the first
phase the factors favouring the reorganization tended
to come into the foreground; in the second phase the
unfavourable factors did so.

The first phase began at the end of 1946 or the
beginning of 1947 with the failure of the negotiations
between East and West, with the obvious impossibility
of achieving real peace, and with the acceptance of a
general situation in world politics which had never
before been accepted in this way—cold war. The cold
war set in at a time when the wounds of the hot war
in Europe had hardly begun to show signs of healing;
indeed the poison in them was threatening the bodies
of whole nations with sepsis. The cold war added a
mortal danger from outside to the danger from within,
and the strategy of the Kremlin welded these two
dangers into a single factor. At this moment the Europeans, for the first time in their history, felt a common

[1] Written in 1953.

131

threat from outside—a totally new experience which forcibly broke through the crust of their usual instincts. At this point, therefore, the tension between East and West became the one fact entirely determining the internal and foreign policies of the free continental nations, and the premises underlying the old European interplay of forces ceased to be effective. In any case, in this first phase there were scarcely any independent powers left to watch one another suspiciously. After the destruction of Germany there was no potential supreme power to arouse fear. There were only tormented populations and anxious governments, fighting for their existence and turning in fear or hope to East or West. *Tertium non datur.* There was no third force to be found between the two world Titans. So the first requirement was to opt, and anyone who wanted to escape the Red flood had to opt for the Anglo-Saxons. America made it easy for those who wished to do so. To begin with at least, they did not have to make any positive contribution, but merely to receive. Their military position was guaranteed by the war potential of the Anglo-Saxons, and their economic position by the unique blood transfusion of the Marshall Plan. In return this plan unequivocally required the future integration of Europe; but the Europeans had no choice. They were patients being kept alive by the American doctor's precious injections and transfusions. They were not in a position to refuse the diet that he was prescribing for the completion of their recovery when the crisis should be safely passed. A team of genuinely convinced statesmen at the head of the old European nations was prepared to undertake a revolutionary recasting of the European system in order to avoid a social revolution. In this situation the peoples' yearning to shake off at last the curse of endless slaughter revived.

Naturally the thoughts concealed behind the veil of rhetorical assurances remained impenetrable. There was certainly no majority in favour of a permanent American hegemony now that the German hegemony had been shaken off. Those who at this moment opted for America did so with reservations; those who were convinced in their renunciation of the old system often hoped that, with American help, they could build on the ruins of obsolete particularism a federated Europe that would develop into a viable third force between East and West, and thus maintain the superiority of the European way of life even against American civilization.

Nevertheless, these visions of a unified Europe could never have captured the imaginations of such wide circles, had the old fear of the danger of a supreme power close at hand not been robbed of significance— if Germany, dismembered, discredited, and formless, had not, to all intents and purposes, ceased to justify any suspicions. Even though she might perhaps, with her unpredictable vitality, rise again one day, this possibility only made it wiser to integrate her within Europe in good time, so that she should not find her way back into the dangerous paths leading to a position of privilege. The spread of the European idea during the first phase was based on three premises: the weakness of the major continental powers, the internal and external threat of Communism, and finally the harmlessness of Germany, both in the present and in the future.

133

As the relationship between these factors changed, the second phase emerged. Where did these changes primarily originate? In America. Paradoxically America's energy in successfully restoring the resilience of Europe's economic and military position had the complicated after-effect of impeding the realization of the European plan instead of furthering it.

The beginning of the Korean war excited a last outburst of panic, comparable with those at the time of the Italian elections, the Berlin blockade, and the Soviet take-over in Czechoslovakia. But the enormous acceleration in American mobilization soon allowed us to breathe again and to take comfort in the belief that the Russian colossus had transferred its attentions to Asia. At the same time the internal threat of Communism began gradually to diminish, as the Marshall Plan cure began to take effect in France and Italy. In Germany, after the currency reform, the Marshall Plan subsidies began the German economic miracle and completed the immunization of the stricken nation against Eastern infiltration, which had in any case had little effect owing to our practical experience of Communism, which was far more eloquent than any propaganda. To sum up: once again free Europe immediately thrust from its consciousness the unfamiliar and painful realization of the common danger from the East, which it had only faced during the brief moment of acute crisis. The pendulum swung back.

Yet did the gradual return of self-confidence and mutual confidence serve the aims of America, whence it came? Did it strengthen the European idea, the realization of which was by no means overwhelmingly in the American interest but even held out to Europe the bait of greater independence from America? On the contrary, the rising constellation moved into the old orbit that had been traced over centuries. It set the old tread-mill of mistrust, to which the nations had been trained by the old system of the balance of power, turning once again. It diverted attention from the problems of world tension, leaving them to the giant states of the world, and fixed attention once more on deep-rooted disputes at home. The recovery of Western Europe, which we owed to America, led to the resurgence of all our old nationalisms.

The same rising tide of public opinion, which now turned with all its old bitterness against neighbouring states, also turned arrogantly on the despised mentor from overseas who was preaching unity. The public now accused him of over-hasty armament, as it had accused him previously of over-hasty disarmament. Was this armament not more than was needed, they asked, and was it not a violation of Russia's reasonable right to security?

But the strongest stimulus towards the old discords lay in the resurgence of Germany.

We have emphasized the fact that our first main factor in modern European history was the fight against the supremacy of any one power, and that the essence of the whole system was concentrated in this factor; for the system was like an arch in a vault, in which every stone has its function in terms of thrust and counter-thrust, but in which it is the key-stone that ultimately holds them together as a vault.

The key-stone here was the fear of hegemony. As soon as the danger of hegemony stirred again, even if only as the remotest of possibilities, a neuralgic spot was touched and Europe's old mentality roused. Our vitality and its miraculous powers of survival revived memories of the horrors of German supremacy, which were part of the recent experience of Western Europe, and overcame the fear of Communist horrors, which the West had never experienced as a reality. The fear in the West was not that Germany might, for a third time, play a dominating role in the world: it would be quite bad enough if she were merely to resume her former privileged position between East and West and take advantage of the tension between the victors, as France had done after the fall of Napoleon. In such a position she would weaken and endanger the West, especially if she were to combine in any way with the Russian peril. Could one expect German nationalism to remain faithful to the West, when in 1945 it had fought on against the West until long after the last stroke of twelve? Was the cry for Europe which, in the first phase, had been most audible in Germany, not essentially the expression of a desire to escape from the ghetto and achieve equality? And even if it was honestly meant, did it not conceal a desire to restore German supremacy in some more acceptable guise? As the value attached by the United States to the military co-operation of the Germany they had only just de-militarized rose, so did our counter-demands and with them, the mistrust of others, especially of our neighbours the French.

There was one counter-demand that was more explosive than all the rest: the demand for German reunification. Here the stimulus that Germany derived from the division of her conquerors found its clearest expression. Our neighbours welcomed our reduction to their own level as a guarantee of their safety, and it was only the use which Russia made of the positions so short-sightedly ceded to her that led the West to realize that it had exchanged Satan for Beelzebub and that there was a danger that the entire territory East of the Iron Curtain, not merely Eastern Germany, might be lost to the West—a particularly terrible prospect when regarded from the Pan-European point of view. Seen in relation to this possibility, the German demand was perfectly justified, as long as it was made by a Germany which shared the Pan-European point of view and was interested in achieving lasting integration. But even in that event, France was afraid that the combination of our irredentist dynamism with American crusading dynamism might involve her in a war with the East which would at best simply restore the dangerous German Reich.

This fear would be even more natural if the demand for re-unification sprang from egocentric nationalism —if it were made without any consideration for Europe and promised to weaken rather than strengthen the unity of the West. If our relationship with the West were to cool, Russia's known desire for security might be satisfied and she might contemplate a peaceful withdrawal from Eastern Germany, but still the result could only be just such a weakening of Western unity. Regardless of whether or not there was any hope of realizing all the beautiful projects that combined Unity, Freedom and Peace and thus logically pressed the victorious world powers who had been our enemies into the service of the impotent loser—so allowing our unprecedented catastrophe to be followed by an unprecedented recovery—it was the spirit of these projects that was in conflict with the idea of European integration. For what would remain of European integration if Germany were to withdraw? The result would be the triumph of the old pattern of dissolution and strife between nations, with unpredictable consequences for the free world and for free Germany too. For today liberty—that is the liberty of the individual, not of the state—can only be preserved as the common property of a consolidated group of nations, and any nation which draws aside to save its own unity will lose it. A hundred years ago the most pressing goal was national unity; for the preservation of freedom offered no problem in the sense in which it does today, whereas unity was the natural demand within that system of nation states which is lying in ruins today. Now, however, after the Third Reich has abused and thrown away our unity by denying freedom, unity must be subordinated to the superior and wider aim of freedom, for today a demand for unity surely has an anachronistic flavour about it. No political watchword can be transplanted into a new situation without carrying with it traces of the soil in which it grew previously.

It is extremely difficult for the remaining free nations of Europe in their changed surroundings to master the anachronistic instincts that they have formed during the centuries of the European system, and the task is hardest of all for the two great neighbours, Germany and France, in whom the continental mentality has crystallized in its most typical form. Both have been prepared to exploit supremacy on a grand scale whenever they have wielded it, and having lost it, have insisted, in moving and tragic tones, on security and equal rights within the system which was to protect them against the supremacy of others. France has not forgotten the *gloire* of the hegemony she herself exercised in previous centuries, and this makes her doubly sensitive to the threat of an hegemony exercised by Germany. Above all, she cannot forget the terrible wounds she has suffered from German supremacy in this century, for Napoleon I and Louis XIV pale beside Hitler. It must cost this ancient nation immense self-discipline to leave its well-worn rut for the path of Western solidarity. No less self-discipline will be required of Germany. She has only just fallen from Satanic heights; she yearns for satisfaction for her injured self-esteem and she is longing for the wounds inflicted by her own struggle for hegemony to heal. Such is the mood in which she is expected to protect her truest interests by soberly recognizing a changed world, and to appreciate the special responsibility she bears to the West as the power that wielded the last and most terrible of all European hegemonies—a responsibility which invests what she does and what she leaves undone with enormous importance. Twice the German nation has failed, like its predecessors, to keep a sense of proportion in its moment of supremacy, but in more highly developed situations and therefore with infinitely more disastrous consequences. If there should ever be a third time, the effects may be more terrible than ever before, and this in spite of Germany's weakness. This very weakness involves us in a special kind of temptation to lose our sense of proportion once again. A loser is far too prone to thrust all his responsibilities upon the shoulders of the victors. He tends too easily to an arrogant, indolent nihilism, to a combination of defiant pride and crippling scepticism. He is tempted to stand aside passively while his own fate is being decided. In the present situation this inability to exercise will-power and a sense of responsibility is characteristic not only of the loser, but also of the victors on the European continent, who are all of course losers at the same time. They too are living in a dream world, a world of make-believe, gazing at the old façade of their independence, but refusing to admit what lies behind it. In the present twilight even their *raisons d'état* are losing their motive force; they no longer edify, nor can they govern the power instincts of individuals or groups. The inner conflict has risen above the level of feelings of mere national community, while it has still not been brought under the healthy control of a feeling of European or Atlantic community. On the contrary, sheltered by American power, European policy is beginning to follow positively parasitical lines. Exploiting the cover offered by American efforts, it is either avoiding efforts of its own, or else directing any efforts it might make towards a purely egocentric particularism—in the vague hope that these puny particularisms may together amount to a third force in the world, between the two giants.

All these complex phenomena can be included within a single concept: the concept of the dying European system. That system is lying in ruins, but its spirit lives on, not so much among statesmen, who have become increasingly like officers without armies, as among their peoples, whose deep-seated instincts protest against the idea that the ruins should be usefully employed to help create a new concept. It is like the pieces of a damaged bridge lying in a river, which obstruct traffic on the water without assisting traffic from one bank to the other.

This interpretation of our situation can be confirmed and illustrated by one of those brief comparisons with classical history which have so often helped us to see our own problems more clearly. I am thinking of the Hellenic system of the *poleis*, which is so illuminating in its basic similarity to the European system, and of the way in which, overshadowed by great powers outside Greece—first Macedon and then Rome—it died a slow death over many centuries. In both cases we find the tenacious but sterile survival of obsolete instincts. We find particularist trends devoid of any sense of proportion, growing ever pettier and ever more outworn, while pursuing their squabbles over scraps of land—the worst possible obstacle to the establishment of a great new order. We find the ghostly repetition of impressive words accompanied by dishonourable actions, or we find a blind reversion into a world of make-believe. We find arrogance and niggardly parasitism side by side. We find the collapse of all sense of community and the degeneration of party and class struggles. The tragedy of the Peloponnesian war for hegemony, with its wholesale self-mutilation, was followed by the bitter satire of endless smaller and ever smaller acts of self-mutilation. The Greeks were actually saved from themselves by the supreme power outside Greece, the philhellene Romans, whose protection allowed the Hellenic spirit to play to an end its great role throughout the *orbis terrarum*, even after the political disintegration of its home.

Black as this picture may appear, one black trait is missing. Hellas did not lie on the frontier of a hostile barbarian world which might attack it if it split up, nor did it possess sufficient weight of its own to upset the structure of the whole *imperium*.

We must be careful not to strain the comparison with details. It will be sufficient if this illuminating reflection of ourselves makes us recognize the specific dangers of our situation and the general concept which characterizes it—the concept of a dying system of states whose spirit survives and whose obsolete conditions threaten to poison the creation of new ones.

Our opening statement that political history still has an important function in the old continent of Europe meant simply this. Its function is no longer to demonstrate the continuity of history, but rather to show the break that has occurred—to knock down what must fall.

EUROPEAN HISTORY TITLES IN
NORTON PAPERBOUND EDITIONS

Aron, Raymond. *On War.* N107

Aron, Raymond. *The Opium of the Intellectuals.* N106

Benda, Julien. *The Treason of the Intellectuals.* N470

Bloch, Marc. *Strange Defeat: A Statement of Evidence Written in 1940.* N371

Brandt, Conrad. *Stalin's Failure in China.* N352

Brinton, Crane. *The Lives of Talleyrand.* N188

Butterfield, Herbert. *The Whig Interpretation of History.* N318

Burn, W. L. *The Age of Equipoise.* N319

Calleo, David P. *Europe's Future: The Grand Alternatives.* N406

Dehio, Ludwig. *Germany and World Politics in the Twentieth Century.* N391

East, W. Gordon. *The Geography Behind History.* N419

Eyck, Erich. *Bismarck and the German Empire.* N235

Ferrero, Guglielmo. *The Reconstruction of Europe.* N208

Feis, Herbert. *Contest Over Japan.* N466

Feis, Herbert. *Europe: The World's Banker 1870-1914.* N327

Feis, Herbert. *The Spanish Story.* N339

Feis, Herbert. *Three International Episodes: Seen from E. A.* N351

Fischer, Fritz. *Germany's Aims in the First World War.*

Gatzke, Hans W. *Stresemann and the Rearmament of Germany.* N486

Gulick, Edward Vose. *Europe's Classical Balance of Power.* N413

Halperin, S. William. *Germany Tried Democracy.* N280

Hobsbawm, E. J. *Primitive Rebels.* N328

Langer, William L. *Our Vichy Gamble.* N379

May, Arthur J. *The Hapsburg Monarchy: 1867-1914.* N460

Menéndez Pidal, Ramón. *The Spaniards in Their History.* N353

Newhouse, John. *Collision in Brussels: The Common Market Crisis of 30 June 1965.*

Nichols, J. Alden. *Germany After Bismarck: The Caprivi Era, 1890-1894.* N463

Rowse, A. L. *Appeasement.* N139

Russell, Bertrand. *Freedom versus Organization: 1814-1914.* N136

Thompson, J. M. *Louis Napoleon and the Second Empire.* N403

Waite, Robert G. L. *Vanguard of Nazism: The Free Corps Movement in Postwar Germany, 1918-1923.* N181

Whyte, A. J. *The Evolution of Modern Italy.* N298

Wolfers, Arnold. *Britain and France between Two Wars.* N343

Wolf, John B. *Louis XIV.*

Wolff, Robert Lee. *The Balkans in Our Time.* N395